Kotel Ha-Ma'aravi (Western Wall)
Churva Square
Ararat Street
Zion Gate
Upper Kollel apartments
King David's Tomb
Diaspora Yeshiva Study Hall
Lower Kollel
Women's Division

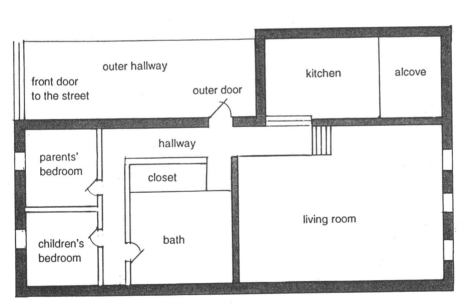

FLOOR PLAN OF THE ARARAT STREET APARTMENT

WHO
BY
FIRE

FELDHEIM PUBLISHERS Jerusalem / New York

WHO BY FIRE

By Chaya Malka Abramson
as told to Esther Tscholkowsky

Photographs: Esther Tscholkowsky 17 *bottom*, 20, 25, 29, 32 *top*, 34 *center*, 36, 39, 144, 155, 156, 172, 176

Library of Congress Cataloging-in-Publication Data

Abramson, Chaya Malka.
Who by fire / by Chaya Malka Abramson and Esther Tscholkowsky.
p.   cm.
ISBN 0-87306-742-8. — ISBN 0-87306-746-0 (pbk.)
1. Abramson, Chaya Malka.   2. Burns and
scalds—Patients–Israel—Biography.   3. Jews—Israel—Biography.
4. Orthodox Judaism—Israel.   I. Tscholkowsky, Esther.   II.Title.
RD96.4.A24   1995
362,1'9711'0092—dc20
[B]   95-41564

First published 1995

FELDHEIM PUBLISHERS
POB 35002/Jerusalem, Israel

200 Airport Executive Park
Nanuet, NY 10954

Typesetting/Layout: Astronel

Printed in Israel

10 9 8 7 6 5 4 3 2

In memory of our dear friend
Alta Chava Hentcha

Acknowledgments

FIRST AND FOREMOST, we thank the Almighty, Who has granted us the gift of his Torah and mitzvot.

We wish to express our gratitude to the following people without whose assistance this book would not have been possible:

— Rabbi and Rebbetzin Goldstein, whose inspiration and guidance are a constant source of Torah growth for ourselves, our families, and our entire community;

— Barbara Sofer, whose many excellent magazine articles served as source material in the research on this book;

— Naomi Harrari, who has been a constant help and inspiration on this project. Her writing and editing skills were much appreciated;

— Shoshana Lepon, our neighbor and friend, who spent many hours of her time reading and offering her professional advice on the manuscript;

— Esther's father, David Charney, who helped edit the final manuscript;

— Naomi Marshall, who helped type the manuscript;

— Yaakov Feldheim and the staff of Feldheim Publishers in Jerusalem whose professional work has brought this book to fruition: Marsi Tabak, Harvey Klineman, Joyce Bennett, Bracha Steinberg, Ruchi Kovall, and Dvora Rhein;

— and the women of the Yeshiva community, who gave freely of their time to be interviewed.

To the hard-working and dedicated doctors and staff

7

of the Hadassah Ein Kerem Hospital Burn Unit and the Hadassah Mt. Scopus Hospital Rehabilitation Center in Jerusalem, whom the Almighty sent to assist in the miracle of my recovery, I offer my profound thanks.

We are especially grateful to our parents, husbands, and children, who willingly encouraged us and helped us throughout the years it took to complete this book.

C.M.A.
E.T.

Preface

I SAT ACROSS FROM Chaya Malka in our shared Mount Zion courtyard and looked at her beautiful yet scarred face. I had known her for many years as a neighbor and friend — before, during, and after her ordeal. Chaya Malka had saved her children and her grandmother from the fire that raged in their apartment in the Jewish Quarter of the Old City of Jerusalem. The fire, like a stone thrown onto the calm mirror-like surface of a lake, caused concentric rings to extend ever outwards: the outer rings were the Yeshiva community and *Am Yisrael*; the inner ones, her immediate family and personal friends. From all over Israel, Europe, the United States, and Canada we had prayed for her recovery.

The fire touched many lives. It touched mine. For her children's sake and for future generations, I wanted the story told. I felt that her miraculous recovery, her inner strength, and her unyielding belief in the Almighty would surely inspire others as they had inspired me.

This is her story as she related it to me. It took us many years and long hours to put it down on paper. Sometimes we laughed; often we cried. It is hoped that this book will strengthen the faith of those who read it, enlighten them to the feelings of those in need, and encourage them to extend the hand of *chesed.* Most of all, Chaya Malka and I wanted to show the important role which the mitzvot of Prayer, Charity, and Repentance play in changing the most difficult of decrees.

E. Tscholkowsky

Introduction

WHY DID ALL THE righteous people in the Torah have such difficult lives? If they were *tzaddikim*, why didn't Hashem bless them with lives of ease and tranquillity? This question is addressed by both the *Midrash Tanchuma* and the *Midrash Rabbah*.

Hashem said to No'ach, "Come you and all your family into the ark, for I have seen you righteous before me in this generation" (*Bereshit* 7:1).

Where does No'ach's righteousness lead him? Into an ark crowded with fierce animals whom he must feed and care for. True, he and his family were saved from destruction, but for all his merit he was given not a moment's peace.

Avraham proved himself righteous throughout nine tests of faith, yet we read in *Bereshit* 21:1, "And it was after these things that Hashem tested Avraham." What was Avraham given after passing nine tests? One more test! And this, the tenth, was the most difficult of all: to be willing to sacrifice his precious son Yitzchak, the progenitor of the Jewish people.

Indeed, we read in *Tehillim* 11:5: "Hashem tests the righteous one, while the wicked one loves violence — this one Hashem's soul despises." It is the *tzaddik* who is tested while the wicked person is left alone!

The Midrash explains this dilemma with three examples — a flax-maker with his flax, a potter with his pots, and a farmer with his oxen.

Flax is a fiber which improves in value when it is well

pounded. Good quality flax is strengthened, purified and made more beautiful under pressure. If the fibers are of poor quality, however, they will become damaged and fall apart. Therefore, the flax-maker will not waste his efforts in beating low-grade flax. He chooses only the finest for his work.

In the same way, Hashem knows that only the righteous will benefit from trials and hardship. They'll be purified from any sins they may have done (for there is no *tzaddik* in the world who does only good and no bad), and they will develop their inner strengths.

Just as a flax-maker pounds his flax, so does a potter beat on his pots, but his purpose is quite different. The potter takes his best pots and strikes them, not to improve them but to demonstrate their quality. If he were to pound on a poorly made pot it would shatter in his hands, and then who would buy his wares?

So, too, when Hashem wants to demonstrate the glory of His creatures. He chooses His "best pots" — His *tzaddikim.* When a righteous person emerges from trials and tribulations with his faith intact, it is a great *kiddush Hashem* — a sanctification of Hashem's Holy Name. People say, "Without the strength of faith in Hashem, no human being could endure such hardship!" Now, a wicked person does no honor to Hashem when he is tested. He may crumble under the pressure or lash out angrily at Hashem and increase his evil.

In the case of the farmer and his oxen, he will choose only the strong beast to bear the yoke. This one does the work of the weaker ones, and shoulders the entire burden of his master. And so it is with us: the righteous bear responsibility for their society, and their deeds bring merit to all.

Chaya Malka truly exemplifies these three concepts.

First, she reached a high level of faith in Hashem and commitment to a Torah life through the struggles she endured. Second, she caused a great *kiddush Hashem* by exhibiting such trust and acceptance. And third, she was the catalyst for many to perform acts of *chesed,* for her and her family. People all over the world were moved to pray for her and open their hearts to the Almighty. People were inspired to give charity, to do many mitzvot and good deeds. Indeed, by bearing her burden with faith, and by fighting so valiantly for her life and the lives of her loved ones, Chaya Malka was able to bring merit to an entire generation.

Rabbi Dr. M. Goldstein
Diaspora Yeshiva

Even there Your hand would lead me,
and Your right hand would hold me.

Ibn Ezra comments: "Your right hand would
hold me" — I am confident that wherever I go,
Your right hand, the symbol of kindness and
mercy, will assist me in all of my endeavors.

 IT WAS AN ORDINARY day in my Mount Zion apartment, if living in an eight-hundred-year-old stone Crusader inn atop King David's Tomb could ever be called ordinary. As I hung the laundry on a line stretched between two rough-hewn stone walls, I thought back to the strange path that had brought me here. Six years had passed since Miriam, my only sibling, had talked me into joining her on a trip through Europe. Miriam had been working as a registered nurse for some time while I had been studying fine art and fashion design in New York. We were both single. I agreed to take a break from it all and see the world with her.

When we were passing through Italy, I remember how one day we happened upon an ancient village nestled in the hills. The narrow, winding, cobblestone streets, the brightly colored laundry scattered about on clotheslines spanning old stone buildings, the special light of the Mediterranean sunshine, made an impression on me. This strange scene was so foreign, and yet so appealing to us, two nice middle-class girls from Waterbury, Connecticut. We had never seen anything like it, yet we both had the same thought: How we'd love to live in a place like this someday! Little did we imagine that less than a year later

A view of our crusader fortress home as it appeared in 1851. The
arrow points to the windows of our apartment.

Simcha renovating our apartment on Mount Zion just before we
moved in.

we would both be married and living next door to each other in a place called Mount Zion, that closely resembled that Mediterranean town.

My dreams had come true. We weren't in Italy, but in our own ancient homeland, living in an ancient stone Crusader inn which was perched atop the tomb of David, King of Israel.

All the money I had saved up over the years in my Waterbury savings account went to renovate the two abandoned rooms with domed ceilings which my husband and I had been allocated as a newly married couple of the Diaspora Yeshiva.

Right outside of King David's Tomb, a dark, enclosed staircase of stone wound up and out onto a narrow corridor which served as a courtyard between several abandoned rooms. The stone steps had been polished down to a slippery shine by hundreds of years of footsteps. Sharing our narrow corridor were four other young families like ourselves, including my sister and her husband, whose apartment was literally on the other side of the wall. We were all new immigrants, newly Observant, and newly married. Most of us had no family in Israel. We supported each other emotionally and shared our happy occasions as well as our difficulties. That made it possible to live in cramped and dilapidated ancient quarters.

Our Yeshiva, following the Musar Movement,* assigned students membership to a specific *"Musar Vaad"* from the time we came into the dormitories as single students and continuing on after marriage. These were support groups, one of the many innovative ideas that our Rabbi had introduced into the Yeshiva. Little did I know then that the deep friendships I formed in those early days in my group would help carry me through the trials to come.

---

* The movement founded by Rabbi Yisrael Salanter in the 19th century, which stressed moral discipline and Torah ethics and values.

Each group of three to five women (the men had their own groups) met once a week. We would talk of how we, with all the "baggage" we carried from our former lives, could get closer to our Creator. We all wanted to change and improve our *middot*, whether that meant having more compassion for others, being more organized in our personal lives, or having more patience with our small children. Our Sages teach that it could take a lifetime to change one personality trait for the better. Our quest required patience, perseverance, good advice, and constant support while keeping our long-term goals constantly in mind. Our group was a sounding board and think tank for each individual in the group in relation to herself and to others. It was a place one did not have to maintain a façade and could air her feelings in an atmosphere of trust. Finding that others had the same difficulties or doubts helped us to accept ourselves and find solutions together.

As my new life unfolded, I found pieces of the puzzle slowly fitting together. Through the sessions we spent in the group we learned how to be good neighbors as well as true friends. Sometimes it wasn't easy knowing what to do or say in certain situations. Should one tell a neighbor she could be heard singing in the shower? How should one teach little children the concept of privacy and knocking on a door before they enter? As we struggled with the trials of daily living, our relationships deepened through the *vaad* and we grew to be an extended family.

Every month we attended a *Rosh Chodesh shiur* for married couples in the *beit knesset*. The Rabbi would speak to us about educating our children, increasing our own learning time and that of our husbands, and how to maintain *sh'lom bayit* — a peaceful atmosphere in the household. We learned to do unconditional *chesed* for one another as we lovingly built our homes.

The Jerusalem sun shone brightly as I stood at the

clothesline hanging up my year-old baby's sleeper, and my thoughts wandered to the future: how my little children, Devorah, Yehoshua (Shua), and baby Esther, would grow up to be part of our vibrant center of Torah teaching and inspiration on Mount Zion; how our little group of families would grow into a large Torah community.

Suddenly I heard shouts from below. My husband Simcha was calling my name. "Malka, Malka!" he gasped as he ran into the house clutching a piece of paper. "It's an eviction notice from the municipality!" He showed me the official looking document. "It says that the City building inspectors have determined that there is an impending danger of this old structure collapsing, and so the City is evicting us from our homes. We have three days to get out!" About a month earlier, we had heard that the inspectors had discovered a crack running through the foundation, rendering our building unsafe. The news had

The vertical crack running through the ancient crusader structure.

surprised us, but we didn't really believe we would ever
have to move because of it. The Yeshiva had called in
other construction engineers for a second opinion, and
they had reassured us that the building could safely stand
another hundred years. And yet now, with a stroke of
the City architect's pen, my dreams were crossed off,
canceled.

I was shocked. I had never imagined we would have
to leave at all, and certainly not so abruptly. As Simcha
hurried to knock on doors to share the news, I stood
frozen, looking past my hanging clothes to the towering
church and the adjacent minaret looming above me. My
mind traveled back to the first time I came to Mount Zion.

Our coming to Israel must have been due to the merit
of our forefathers — but Miriam and I always said it
was due to Nana, the matriarch of our family. A great-
grandmother to our children and a very dear person to
us, she had made it possible for the two of us to visit
Israel that first time on our way through Europe. "Go to
Israel!" were her firm instructions. "Make sure it is part
of your travel plans," she had insisted as she slipped an
extra $350 into each of our handbags. It was the push in
the right direction that we needed.

We didn't know much about Israel, and especially
about the world of Orthodox Judaism, yet in our complete
ignorance, we both ended up at a Yeshiva. It was late
Wednesday night when we finally arrived at Jerusalem's
Central Bus Station with our hand luggage and a little
note that said: *For a great Shabbos, stop off at the Diaspora
Yeshiva.* The note had been given to us by a woman friend
with whom we had traveled.

As soon as we alighted from our inter-city bus, we
headed straight for a public phone and called the Yeshiva.
The phone was answered by a very friendly secretary,
who invited us to come right over. She started to give us
careful directions to the bus that would take us there, and

then suddenly she stopped. "On second thought," she said, "I don't like the idea of two young girls wandering alone at night in the Old City. Do me a favor, take a taxi and I'll pay for it." We gladly agreed to do so and went to find a cab.

❄ ❄ ❄

As our taxi slowly wound its way up the dark and deserted dirt road to Mount Zion, we wondered with trepidation where we were being taken. The night was chilly and the wind was strong. Much to our relief, when we got to the top of the hill there was a woman there, smiling and signaling us to stop. "Hi, girls! I'm Susan Leibman, the Yeshiva secretary you spoke to on the phone," she reassured us. "I hope it wasn't too difficult getting here." She paid the driver his fare, and we stepped out of the cab and into her welcoming arms. The night had suddenly become friendly. The air was filled with the strong fragrance of unknown flowers. Even though it must have been well past office hours, Mrs. Leibman seemed pleased to have waited for us. We told her a little about ourselves as we followed her further up the hill.

"I'm Miriam," my sister said, "and this is Malka." I smiled and nodded, adding, "*Na'im me'od* — nice to meet you. Since we've come to Israel we've been using our Hebrew names."

Mrs. Leibman smiled at us over her shoulder. We reached a sturdy iron gate which led into a quaint courtyard lined with trees. Entering behind her, we stepped into an ancient, brightly lit building. What topped off this strange and wonderful scene was that the thick stone walls and the high, arched ceilings of the huge room seemed to be vibrating from the lively music of what sounded like a rock concert that was going on!

"These kids are all my 'boys' and part of the Diaspora Yeshiva Band," she told us proudly. "They're playing here for a group of Israeli soldiers. You can see for yourself how our soldiers are enjoying themselves, singing along with the music."

As we walked further into the hall, Mrs. Leibman pointed out to us some of her "girls," who were also enjoying the concert. The young women, dressed in long skirts with colorful scarves on their heads, came over and showed us where to sit. As soon as Mrs. Leibman was reassured that we were in good hands, she left for home. Although we didn't get to talk to those young women very much that night, we would soon all become close friends.

After the concert was over, a tall, nice-looking young man with a red beard graciously stepped forward and took our bags. I never imagined then that in the not-too-distant future he was to become my brother-in-law. Miriam and I looked at each other. "Hey, this seems like a really interesting place," Miriam said. "Let's stay a while." We had anticipated that Shabbat would be the "unforgettable experience" our friend had described; in fact, the excitement had begun the moment we arrived.

We walked together to the girls' dormitories in the Jewish Quarter of the Old City, adjacent to Mount Zion, under a moonless sky. Instead of sleeping, we stayed up late that night talking with some of the girls who were staying there. They were to be my roommates during the time I would be living in the dorms. In the course of the evening, one of the girls described to us the many travelers who had passed through Mount Zion and the Yeshiva in the time she had been here. Some stayed a day, some a week, some a month. Some, like herself, had stayed for a year and made it their home. I wondered what kind of traveler I would be.

I suddenly remembered how, as a teenage girl, I used to enjoy sitting next to my parents in synagogue, even though I did not understand the Hebrew words in the prayer book. I would flip to the back of the book and read a certain prayer in English that spoke about Mount Zion. The image of Mount Zion was like a thread weaving its way throughout the text. Years later I realized how that far-off place had seemed to speak to my soul, but only now was its special meaning in my life being realized.

※　※　※

As guests of the dormitory, we were invited to attend classes the next day at the Women's Division of the Yeshiva. In the early morning, the girls (as we called each other, even though some of us were in our twenties and thirties) in the dorm escorted us back to Mount Zion from the Jewish Quarter. The view from the road was breathtaking, as we had missed seeing anything in the dark when we'd walked there the night before. The girls served as tour guides, explaining the history of the Jewish Quarter and of the Armenian Quarter which borders on it. The extraordinary sight of the Mount of Olives cemetery loomed in the distance and we could see the hills of Moav in Jordan, the Dead Sea, and the Judean Hills to our right. As the Jewish Quarter was under construction* in those days, donkeys burdened with stones and debris were everywhere. Their Arab drivers loaded them up, and then unloaded the sacks outside the city walls. The paths were not wide enough for vehicular traffic. We passed through Zion Gate and, turning to the right, continued down a very narrow dirt road which was bordered on either side by the high walls of a church.

As we made our way down a steep incline along the side of Mount Zion, one of the girls explained to us what she had learned about the area. Although we had been

---

* Between 1948 and 1967, the Jewish Quarter was in Jordanian hands, during which time they reduced most of the residences and historic sites, including many ancient synagogues, to rubble. After the Six-Day War, the Jewish Quarter was reconstructed and restored.

Mount Zion as it appears from the Yemin Moshe windmill.

traveling around the country for a month, it was my first real historical sightseeing tour in Israel, so I was eager to hear.

"Before 1967, Mount Zion was an Israeli army base," she said, "situated on the 'Green Line,' the old border separating Israel from the Kingdom of Jordan. Israeli soldiers stationed in the abandoned houses there protected Jewish Jerusalem from the hostile Jordanian soldiers stationed on the city ramparts. The only way for Jews to catch a glimpse of their beloved Western Wall and Temple Mount, which were situated in the captured and sealed-off Jewish Quarter, was by climbing this very steep mountain pathway up Mount Zion and continuing up onto the roof over King David's Tomb. After the Six-Day War and the liberation of the Jewish Quarter from Arab hands, the dream of praying at the Western Wall was realized and Mount Zion lost its flow of pilgrims. The only sound that was heard was that of the brokenhearted, who would come to recite *Tehillim* at King David's Tomb.

"After the evacuation of the army," she continued, "the director of the Ministry of Religion wanted to emphasize and develop the spiritual quality of this holy Mount Zion which had been neglected after serving as an Israeli army post from 1948 to 1967. Just as King David had used his energies to inspire the hearts of the Jewish people to return to their Creator, it seemed especially appropriate that Mount Zion, the site of King David's Tomb, should be used as a center for the return of wandering Jewish souls."

Shortly after the Six-Day War, he had entrusted Rabbi Dr. Mordecai Goldstein, *shlita*, with the task of establishing a Yeshiva on Mount Zion. The Rebbe (as his students lovingly call him), had learned for twenty years under Rabbi Chenoch Leibowitz, *shlita*, the *Rosh Yeshivah* of Yeshiva Chofetz Chaim in New York. He soon attracted a group of American students who were drawn to his dynamic learning style, based on intense rabbi-student interaction. He felt it was his mission to bring Torah learning to everyone, no matter what their background.

As my new friend spoke, I realized that I was one of those souls seeking their Jewish roots.

As we reached the bottom of the hill, we stood for a moment and looked across at the panoramic view of the Yemin Moshe neighborhood, with its famous windmill overlooking the Gei-Hinnom Valley. At the very foot of the hill stood a simple abandoned looking one-story stone structure. We were quite surprised at the sight, since no one had described the school to us. As we walked into our classroom and sat down on a hard wooden bench, we noticed the absence of electricity, windows, and running water. Yet a beautiful radiance flooding from several skylights on the ceiling bathed the vast mahogany table in the center of the room with light. Ten girls seated together on either side of the table seemed oblivious to the relative harshness of their surroundings as they listened attentively to their teacher.

One of the most impressive classes I attended during that first day was the Rabbi's weekly class for women on the Midrash for the weekly Torah portion. It became

a favorite of mine. There were some brilliant students
who would always have a dialogue with the Rabbi about
different parts of "the puzzle." The segment of Midrash
was called "the piece." He would ask us, "How does this
piece affect women today?" and he always made the piece
relevant to our lives. The material somehow would evoke
profound personal feelings that resulted in questions,
thoughts, and sometimes tears. I was not accustomed
to such openness at first, and in a classroom setting
exclusively for women, but this was our time with the
Rabbi, our opportunity to learn and grow. If one had
difficulty in understanding something, this was the time
to raise it; maybe others were troubled by the same thing.
I felt privileged to be a part of such an amazing group
of brave women who were striving for understanding of
themselves and seeking truth.

After that first night of staying up in the dorms, Miriam
and I didn't get much chance to talk to each other. Each
day was packed with stimulating, mind-boggling concepts
that affected the very core of our lives. We were swept
away in a whirlwind of new experiences and activities.

About two weeks later, at an unusually quiet moment,
we found ourselves alone together and Miriam took the
opportunity to discuss what was on her mind. She told
me how she believed that all the new things we had been
learning about the Torah and a true Jewish way of life
were right and that she was ready to commit herself to
taking that path. In other words, she wanted to stay. Well,
I had come to the same conclusion, I confessed. I too was
ready to stay. I felt the Yeshiva environment was intense
and sincere. It exemplified all the things I really cared
about in life. All the unanswered questions I had placed in
the back of my mind were starting to be answered; it all
made sense. Yes, I said, this was for me! We hugged each
other and hurried to write our parents the good news.

Receiving our letter back in Waterbury, Connecticut,

our parents were stunned to hear that we wanted to
stay in Israel. Mom and Nana, as the family emissaries,
jumped on the first plane to see for themselves just what
was really going on. It was hard for them to believe that
Miriam and I were making the same decisions at the same
time. "How could one place satisfy both their individual
desires," Mom wondered, "especially after they had been
going in such different directions in their lives!"

❋   ❋   ❋

Nana and Mom took us on a two-day trip to the Galilee
to have some private time with us and try to persuade us
to come home and think over our "rash decision." When
we instructed them to cash in our two return tickets,
they were incredulous. After a three-week visit and many
heart-to-heart discussions, they returned home without
us. Mom did not understand exactly what was happening,
but slowly she and Dad got used to the idea that we were
here to stay. Our previous American Jewish lives made
me think of a glass-bottomed boat that I had seen in Eilat:
Jewish holidays and customs were visible but distant from
us, as if separated by a sheet of glass. We could see their
beauty but could not really feel them. Now it was as if
we had jumped into the teeming waters of our new/old
heritage. Diving right in, we discovered, is the only way to
really experience the sea of Torah!

Not long after that visit, our parents received a phone
call from Miriam telling them of her engagement to one
of the American Yeshiva students she had met. Ben Zion,
a dentist from Los Angeles, had arrived at the Yeshiva
a year before we did. The dedication and sincerity of the
students he met had convinced him to give studying
Torah a try. Soon after meeting Miriam, Ben Zion realized
that they had a lot in common. Both were in the medical
profession and both had enjoyed traveling through many
countries on their way to Israel. They shared the desire to

My sister and brother-in-law sitting in their apartment next door to ours, on Mount Zion.

build a traditional Jewish home together. Miriam begged our parents and grandmother to come back again for the wedding, and they did. My sister had a beautiful *Lag ba-Omer* wedding in the *beit knesset* of the Yeshiva. How happy we were that Mom and Dad and Nana could all be with us for such a joyous occasion.

As usual, the Yeshiva's band helped to make the wedding especially lively. Rabbi Goldstein understood that the soul of the younger generation was deeply tied to music. He encouraged his students to take whatever talents they had developed before they became religious and to use them for Torah. "Take your art and sing of your love for Hashem," he would tell them. "Bring the inspirational words of *Tehillim* into a modern context through music, to open up the souls of other young Jews around you." What better place could there be to play such music than close by the tomb of the "sweet singer of Israel," King David, composer of *Tehillim.*

As the first "religious rock band," the Diaspora Yeshiva

Band created a new category of music. Three years after its formation, the band competed against big-name Israeli performers in the Chasidic Song Festival of 1978 and won the contest with the beautiful song "*Malchus'cha*," taken from King David's psalms.

A few days after Miriam's wedding, my father and I were sitting outside the courtyard of King David's Tomb, at the festive Saturday night *Melaveh Malkah* concert. One of the musicians in the band was playing the clarinet before a young and lively audience. Men and boys broke into a spontaneous dance up front near the stage, as the women, in a secluded area, danced with equal enthusiasm.

Dad leaned over and, putting his arm around me, whispered in my ear. "Are you sure there isn't someone here tonight for you?" Mom had overheard Dad's query and the two of them looked at me questioningly.

"Try not to stare," I whispered back, "but you see that clarinet player up there?"

My parents nodded and smiled. "Maybe we could make another wedding before we leave?" Dad suggested. "I can't afford to come back again this year."

"Oh, Dad," I said, blushing deeply at the idea.

It wasn't until months later, however, that our friends encouraged Simcha, the very clarinet player I had pointed out to my parents, to ask me out and at the same time encouraged me to go out with him. Simcha had rediscovered his musical talents at the Yeshiva, where he played clarinet at the *Melaveh Malkah* concert every Saturday night. Studying philosophy at Tel Aviv University had pushed his thoughts towards discovering Hashem and the purpose of life. Eventually, he had decided to follow two close friends to the Diaspora Yeshiva.

One of the main attractions of the Yeshiva for Simcha was Rabbi Goldstein, the *Rosh Yeshivah*. His strength of personality was evident as he answered all of Simcha's questions honestly and in a straightforward manner.

Unashamed to express his strong opinions, he attracted many students with his personal warmth and challenged their assumptions. He treated each young Jew as part of his own family.

The Rabbi's method was to take a new student, no matter what his background, and put him straight into an English-speaking Gemara study session. There the student would open a Gemara and start learning with his teacher and peers on his own level. The Rabbi believed that love of Torah did not come through introductory courses or lectures on Jewish philosophy, but rather from the students themselves grappling with the brilliant minds of our Torah Sages.

Simcha was fascinated with the new world that had opened up for him and decided to try out the life of Torah Judaism. Did the shoe fit? Yes, and the wedding ring he slipped on my finger fit perfectly, too. Well, there had indeed been two weddings that first year, and my parents and Nana had all attended. My mother and grandmother actually came three times that year. Even though Miriam and I were both married now, it was a long while before my father stopped asking, "Now, when are you girls coming home?"

For Simcha's parents, however, his decision to settle in Israel did not come as a surprise. Evelyn and Sam Abramson had raised their sons with a love of Israel and a deep commitment to the Jewish people. Sam, a dynamic force in the United Jewish Appeal organization, spared no effort towards furthering the development of Israel. Sam had an abiding interest in Jewish life the world over which was expressed in the book he wrote, *Jewish Landmarks in Europe*. As part of his job, my father-in-law would accompany many UJA missions to Israel each year. On one of these trips before 1967, he had led his group up the winding cobblestone path of Mount Zion, passing the same little building which would house our Women's

The Diaspora Yeshiva Band before their Saturday night concert.

Simcha and I pose
for a wedding portrait
on the steps leading
to our apartment.

Division in the years to come. They continued up the road alongside thousands of other Jewish pilgrims from all over the world, until they reached the observation post over King David's Tomb. From this rooftop, visitors had a fine view of the Western Wall and the Old City, which Jews could not enter.

"For more than a thousand years," Sam had explained to his tour group each year, "Jewish tradition has identified Mount Zion as being the last resting place of King David and his descendants, the Kings of Yehudah. Benjamin of Tudela, the fearless Jewish traveler who visited Jerusalem in the twelfth century, describes in his journal how royal graves were discovered here when a church collapsed. Workmen who went further into the caves to steal the treasures they saw, were driven back by a powerful and mysterious wind. Fainting from fright, they regained consciousness to hear a menacing voice warning them to leave. Towards the end of the nineteenth century, non-Moslems were allowed access only to the rooms above the tomb. For the Festival of Shavuot, the traditional anniversary of King David's passing, the British Mandate allowed Jews closer access. After the War of Independence in 1948, Mount Zion was in the Israeli section of Jerusalem and the Royal Tomb became a focus of pilgrimage."

To think that his son was living at this very historical site so many years later! And this was our backyard, where our children would ride their tricycles and we would build our *sukkah* and hang our laundry. I lifted up the empty laundry basket in a daze and slowly walked back into the apartment that I would soon have to abandon. Placing the basket on the kitchen table, I sat down dejectedly. I looked up at our high-domed ceiling and down at the star pattern of the old stone floor tiles which extended out to the borders of the room. A black metal spiral staircase which we had installed ascended to our sleeping loft. The loft was suspended over a small addition we had

34

Grandma Evelyn (Simcha's mother), baby Esther, and I at our annual
Women's Sukkot Brunch, a few weeks before the fire.

Simcha and I with
our first child, Devorah.

Simcha, Devorah, and Shua
sitting on the stone steps
that led up to the roof.

built onto the original room. I stood up and walked into the second domed-ceiling room where our children slept. Sitting down under the arch of the inset window seat, I looked out below onto the courtyard of King David's Tomb as I tried to collect my thoughts.

We were idealistic American kids with ambitious goals. We were willing to give up the material comforts with which we had been raised because we saw beauty, truth, and purity in a Torah-true life. Torah and mitzvot were first on our list of priorities. We were satisfied with much less material comfort than our parents' generation would have found acceptable. We are taught that Mount Sinai, the smallest, most humble mountain around, was where the Torah was given to *Bnei Yisrael.*

We were conscious of our vital role in ensuring a Jewish presence on Mount Zion, amid the churches and Arab cemeteries. On Friday night my husband would raise his voice to recite Kiddush so that we could hear the words over the clanging of the church bells. In the mornings I would be awakened by deafening carillons at 5:00 A.M. I would look out to see the bellringer climbing the tower above our window. Despite the deafening racket we somehow adjusted to the hourly chimes which shook the walls of our little house. On the High Holy Days of Rosh Hashanah and Yom Kippur we would join our Yeshiva community for the services held in King David's Tomb. It was not easy to concentrate on *Kol Nidrei* with the Christian pilgrims singing hymns right above us in The Last Supper Room!

We would often climb up onto the roof which offered a panoramic view of the Old City of Jerusalem, the Mount of Olives, and the Judean Hills. Below in the courtyard of King David's Tomb, Simcha played clarinet in the Saturday night concerts. My window seat directly above the courtyard allowed me to enjoy the show in comfort. Busloads of tourists would arrive and Rabbi Goldstein's

From the window I could see the Melaveh Malkah concert every Saturday night.

words came back to me: "Watch," he said. "Eventually the whole world will come to Mount Zion." And, it seemed, they did — in saris, kimonos, jahlabiyas, colorful turbans, and sombreros. Endless streams of tourists speaking many strange tongues passed beneath my window.

Just as I had been a curious tourist passing through that small Italian town years before, so was I now the object of curiosity for tourists passing through Mount Zion. "What's this!" they demanded to know as they peeked in through our window curtains. One morning there had been a knock on our door, and before I could protest, a mustached, debonair Arab gentleman in a cream-colored suit, accompanied by his fashionably dressed wife and two friends, marched into my living room. "Look," he told his companions, "this is where I played as a child with my brothers." He introduced himself as someone whose family cemetery had been on Mount Zion for generations. His departure was as sudden and swift as his entry had been. It was obvious that this well-to-do Arab could not bear the close confines of his childhood home for more than a few moments.

Meeting this former occupant of my home face to face made me wonder about my justification for living here. I delved into the history of the area and learned that Simcha and I, my sister and her husband, and a handful of other families were the first Jewish residents on Mount Zion since the Ramban in the 13th century. Rabbi Moshe ben Nachman, known as the Ramban or Nachmanides, was born in Spain where he became famous as a great Talmudic scholar and Biblical commentator. After winning a much publicized debate with the church, he was expelled to Eretz Yisrael, and there he remained until his death in 1270. We were pioneers building our homes in the same location where the Ramban had reorganized the Jewish community on Mount Zion before relocating to the Jewish Quarter. In the era of the Crusades, 800 years ago, our new home had provided lodging for pilgrims who had been locked out of the Old City walls. Indeed, I could still see the round hooks embedded in the stone walls where travelers had tied up their horses.

In 1187 the triumphant Saladin, the sultan of Egypt whose personal physician was Rabbi Moses ben Maimon, known as the Rambam or Maimonides, rescued Jerusalem from the grip of the Crusaders. The Jews were then allowed to reenter Jerusalem. Local legend tells how the sultan demonstrated his gratitude to the five Arab conquering generals by presenting them with sections of Jerusalem. The first four generals each chose a quarter of the Old City and the fifth took Mount Zion. At the beginning of the 16th century, Eretz Yisrael was conquered by the sultan Suleiman the Magnificent, ruler of the Ottoman Empire, and it became another part of the Turks' rapidly expanding domain. Suleiman commissioned two architects to rebuild Jerusalem's city walls with explicit instructions to include Mount Zion within their perimeter. Despite his instructions, however, Mount Zion was overlooked and remained outside the walled city. The architects paid for their mistake with their lives: their tombs can be found today, right inside the walls near Jaffa Gate. The descendants of the fifth general continued to live on Mount Zion until 1948.

During Israel's War of Independence in 1948, the local Arabs fled Jerusalem, obeying the orders of their leaders. They had hoped to return after Israel was conquered by the invading Arab armies, but to their surprise and dismay the Jews won the war and a new state, the State of Israel, was established. The Arabs stayed away despite the pleas of the victorious Jewish leaders for them to return in peace, thereby relinquishing any claim to their former homes.

From 1948 until we had come to settle here, these rooms remained abandoned and in ruins. Young *kollel* couples spent weeks clearing out the rubble, reconstructing walls, and installing modern conveniences such as electricity, plumbing, window frames, and doors. Uncovering each old stone tile buried under the rubble was an exciting adventure. We cleaned out these rooms and set up our new homes.

We were forming the foundation of a new community; but what could we give our children if we were ignorant? Having little babies did not stop us from attending the Women's Division sessions daily. Some women even brought their newborns to class. The babies were often distracting and noisy, but it was worth it. The Rabbi assured us that we would appreciate our husband's Torah learning more with the knowledge and love of Torah we gained at the Women's Division. We were learning to look at life and to live it through a Torah perspective.

The Yeshiva was situated on the eastern slope of Mount Zion, with the students, staff, and married couples (the *kollel*) living in various buildings scattered across the slope. One of the main concentrations of housing was in the Crusader fortress above King David's Tomb. Here the

We often clung to one another as we made our way through the dark narrow corridors which led past King David's Tomb.

A last picture of our apartment on Mount Zion: the day of the eviction.

"upper *kollel*," as we were fond of calling it, lived. Further down the slope in relatively newer buildings (only around 200 years old) lived another nine families we called the "lower *kollel*." The main road separating these two areas led to the Yeshiva's *beit knesset,* office and study halls.

My friends who lived in the lower *kollel* would often visit me upstairs. We loved to talk until late into the night, after the kids were asleep. When it was time to leave I would accompany them down the pitch-black, winding stairwell and out through the narrow corridors which led past King David's Tomb onto the main road. Often as we clung to one another, I was reminded of the palpable darkness of Egypt. When we finally reached the lower *kollel,* my friends would anxiously insist on accompanying me back to my house, but I always declined their offer, reassuring them that I would be fine since I knew my way so well I could manage even with my eyes closed. I could not imagine living anywhere else — but now we were being evicted!

The news of the eviction spread like wildfire. From that moment on there was a frantic rush to find alternative housing. Where would we go? Everyone began looking for available apartments. We were all packing our belongings into boxes and saying goodbye to the homes we had built together. The Jewish Quarter of the Old City was our natural choice, since we wanted to be close to our community and to our Yeshiva. My husband and I scoured the Jewish Quarter for a place for our family. At that time there were only three apartments available for rent: the first had absolutely no room for our wide American stove; in the second, our American appliances couldn't even fit through the kitchen door. The third was still not ideal, but it was better than none. As one entered the ground-floor apartment, immediately to the left was a huge sunken living room wth three large windows. To the left of the living room was a kitchen roomy enough to accommodate our oversized American appliances. Two small bedrooms and a bathroom were separated from the rest of the apartment by a long hallway to the right of the front doorway. Even though it was situated right next to the Armenian Quarter and the Arab shuk, and had no courtyard for the kids to play in, the place felt comfortable and spacious.

Miriam, who was pregnant at the time, had just gone through a similar ordeal, settling her family in a small apartment around the corner from ours. I felt at least some consolation that Miriam would be close by and that our good friends, Sima and Yehoshua Mann, would be our neighbors three flights up. Maybe we could recreate the feeling of closeness that we had on Mount Zion.

Two years earlier Sima, then a young student in the

Women's Division, had offered to stay over and help me out while Simcha was away on a tour with the band. I had two little babies then and was grateful for any assistance. Sima and I had become close friends during that time. Now as the young wife of Yehoshua Mann, a rabbinical student from our Yeshiva, and the new mother of an infant girl, she still found time to continue learning as she had before she was married.

Although I was relieved thinking we would finally have a normal home with more space and privacy, I would have given it up gladly to be back on Mount Zion.

Not everyone was lucky enough to find a place in time. Shortly after we moved, there was a knock on the door of our former neighbors' apartment on Mount Zion. Two burly men barged in and began hauling out the boxes in their living room, despite our neighbors' outcries, and dumped them at the bottom of the stairwell. They repeated this until all the tenants, their furniture, and all their possessions had been evacuated into the street. Then one of the city officials came and installed a new bolt on the gate, locking the former tenants out of their building forever. Since there were no available apartments on Mount Zion, some of the homeless went to double up with other Yeshiva families who were already living in the Jewish Quarter of the Old City. It was not until weeks later that they were able to find their own accomodations.

I knew I would have to get the house in order as quickly as possible, since Simcha would soon be leaving with the band for their annual winter tour of the U.S. Even though we were not many yards away, the move from Mount Zion outside the Old City walls to the Jewish Quarter inside the Old City walls was like moving from one universe to another.

The Old City was newly rebuilt since its destruction by the Jordanian armies in 1948. Since its recapture and liberation by the Israeli Army in 1967, tremendous effort had been expended restoring the Quarter. About four hundred families had settled there, with one little grocery store which served all the residents. The quaint flavor of the Quarter had been maintained by the architects, who duplicated the ancient stone buildings with their arches, courtyards, and balconies. The narrow streets formed a complex maze of footpaths where no cars were allowed to enter. Preserving and recreating the historic beauty of the Old City meant compromising the needs for twentieth century living. The parking lot, for example, was at least ten minutes away from many homes, which meant getting drenched on a winter day just getting to one's car.

I had so many things to do — I was trying to make some semblance of order, for I wanted to make it more homey for Simcha before he left. Things were going smoothly and I began to feel that maybe this too was for the best, that maybe it wouldn't be so bad after all.

One Friday morning, the week before Simcha left, as I was preparing my gefilte fish for Shabbat, I realized that in all the confusion of moving I had misplaced my pareve pot. "Sima probably has one I could borrow," I thought. "I'll just run up the three flights of stairs and knock on the door." Of course, Sima was happy to lend one to me. I felt the pressure of Shabbat approaching as I noticed the moments ticking away, so I cut our conversation short. "Thanks, Sima. Have a good Shabbos," I said, and I was off. As I reached the top landing, I suddenly closed my eyes. With the pot in one hand and holding onto the banister with the other, I started to go down the stairs, strangely imagining myself having to descend those three flights in the dark. Little did I know this was a premonition of what would take place soon afterwards.

A few days later Simcha bid a tearful goodbye to me and our three small children. Nana, who had been visiting Israel at the time, kindly offered to stay overnight and help out with the kids. She would be leaving the next morning on an early plane back to the United States. Miriam and I had a farewell dinner party in Nana's honor, in a local restaurant and when we returned, Miriam stayed a while to have some tea and cookies. As was usual whenever the three of us got together, Miriam and I started asking Nana to tell us more about her childhood in Hungary. We knew that our great-grandmother had been religious and had covered her hair with a wig. Like excited school children, we anxiously waited to hear all the details of those days, soaking up every word as Nana elaborated on the stories she had told us on her previous visit. As Miriam and I set out the cookies and tea, Nana leaned back on the couch and began.

Nana was the youngest of eleven children. She recalled that when she was six years old, her father would often lie under a big tree in their front yard. He was gravely ill and one time after she had brought him a tray of food, he told her that in the autumn when the leaves fell off the tree, he would also be gone. Nana's eyes filled with

Nana's family's flour mill in Trizes, Hungary.

tears as they did every time she told us the story — and so did ours. This reminiscence evoked another, and then another, recollection of her childhood. It was after her father died that she was sent to live at the home of her aunt, whose wealthy family owned the village flour mill. On *erev Shabbat*, Nana would deliver baskets of freshly baked *challot* and pots of chicken soup to poor families in the village.

"After my aunt died," Nana told us, "her family created 'The Esther F. Sunshine Fund' in her memory. Because my dear aunt was a religious woman who loved to help others, we felt it was appropriate to honor her by visiting the sick and collecting charity to give to the poor."

Nana was seventeen when her sister died and Nana's mother sent her off to marry her sister's husband. All she had thought about was how she would lovingly take care of her sister's orphaned baby girl, with no thought at all for herself.

After we finished our tea, Miriam turned on some music. "Come, Nana, let's dance the Hungarian *chardash*." We danced together for a while, then Miriam tearfully kissed Nana goodbye and left for home. I looked at Nana wistfully, finding it hard to believe she would be back in Florida the next day. Would I ever see her again? I couldn't bear the thought of letting her spend her last night with us sleeping on the couch, as she insisted. "Come on, Nana, isn't this silly?" I coaxed her. "Come sleep in my nice cozy room." But she refused, explaining that she wanted to stay up late packing her suitcase, and didn't want to disturb me. The couch was just fine, she said. It was no use trying to convince her. I knew there would be only a quick goodbye in the morning, so I tried to seize the moment to express my love to this woman who was so very dear to me. We hugged, kissed, and cried. These visits always went by too fast. I really didn't want to say goodbye because I didn't want her to go.

I left Nana standing at the dining room table next to her open suitcase. Now it was time for my nighttime check list: lock the door, turn out the lights, and make sure that the kids were covered well. Jerusalem winter nights were cold, especially in old stone buildings. Then I slipped on a flannel nightgown over my turtleneck shirt and got into bed. After reciting the *Shema* as I did each night, I fell into a sound sleep.

I was brought low but He saved me.
Return to your rest, my soul, for Hashem
has been kind to you.
You delivered my soul from death,
my eyes from tears, my feet from falling.

TEHILLIM 116:6-8

THE APARTMENT was dark when I awoke with a start. "Malka, Malka!" Nana's frightened voice was calling me. "I smell gas!" I leaped out of bed, jammed my feet into my slippers, and sniffed the newly installed gas heater that was suspended on our bedroom wall. There was no odor of gas coming from it. I dashed through the hallway into the children's room and did a quick check of the heater there. I found nothing out of order. I raced down the hallway in the direction of the living room, and saw Nana from the corner of my eye, standing by the door. And then I was stopped dead in my tracks. An invisible wall of gas, the smell of which inundated my whole being, blocked my passage. It transformed reality. I told myself, "Slow down. This is very serious — think fast!"

The odor was overpowering, but I walked right through that wall. I was fighting the undertow of air, or the lack of it, to get through to the gas heater across the room. I didn't have to smell it because the odor was everywhere. "Malka, open the windows!" Nana was frantically calling. She seemed so far away. I stepped towards the closest window, where I hesitated, thinking that perhaps I should close the gas valves first. Instead I followed Nana's urgent plea and flung open the large arched window. Taking another step, I threw open the second window alongside it, then another step and opened the third.

As I turned back to Nana I heard a tremendously loud, echoing noise. It sounded like the "whoosh" of a whip, followed by a blast. Bright yellow dancing flames appeared everywhere, and I was standing in the midst of them. The gas had somehow escaped; a spark from somewhere caused it to ignite.

Images of scenes of someone running through fire wrapped in a blanket flashed across my mind. I looked around — there was nothing to grab to cover myself with. Everything was on fire. I lowered my head, lifted my forearms to protect my face, and ran through the fire, out of the fiery sunken living room and into the hall. As I ran by I caught a split-second glimpse of my poor Nana using her hands to put out burning embers on her body.

The light in the hallway was dim but sufficient for me to see the bed in my tiny bedroom. I dove onto the mattress, rocking to and fro in its soft depths, extinguishing the flames on my body. I succeeded in searing a hole in the mattress and leaving a charred image of myself on the sheets. My blue flannel robe was hanging in the open closet. I jumped up and quickly put it on, since my nightgown had burned up completely.

My first instinct was to call for help, but as I placed my finger on the dial of the phone, I thought to myself, "This is crazy, I have to move! There's no time to call for help and the phone lines are probably melted anyway." I ran into the children's bedroom. Shua was already awake, sitting up in the bottom bunk and coughing. I grabbed him up in my arms. Devorah sat up and started coughing too. I was desperate — I could not manage all the children at once. I forced a smile and with great effort I gently reassured her that everything was all right. "Don't worry," I said. "I'll be right back to get you."

Clutching Shua tightly, I ran down the hallway to the front door, yanked it open and raced through the narrow dark corridor and out of the building. Outside the apartment house people had already begun to gather. I hastily thrust Shua into the arms of a neighbor standing there and ran through the smoke-filled hallway straight back into my children's bedroom. I gently pulled Devorah down from the top bunk bed with my burnt right hand and positioned her on my hip. Baby Esther had already stood up in the corner of her crib and was reaching out for me. I grasped her by the front of her pajama sleeper and lifted her up and out of the crib. Though my hands had been badly burned, the act of lifting my baby was painless and easy. The thought that I might not be able to carry my children out of the burning apartment had not occurred to me.

Outside in the street, in the pre-dawn light, it was bitter cold. I searched the faces in the crowd for Nana, who I had assumed had left the apartment on her own. None of the faces looked familiar. I realized to my horror that she must have remained inside. My throat felt parched as I screamed her name, desperately hoping that she was among the crowd but out of my sight. There was no reply. I thrust the children into someone's arms and raced back inside the building. A man in an army jacket was standing at the front door of my apartment. "Can you go in and get my Nana?" I begged him desperately. He looked in at the blazing apartment and shook his head. I pushed past him and went inside myself.

Instinctively, I knew exactly where Nana would be. I also was aware that the fire was raging in the sunken living room to my left and from what I could see had not yet reached the right side of the apartment where the bedrooms were situated. I ran through the hallway again, this time into my bedroom, and found Nana standing by the open window directly opposite the doorway, badly burned and breathing heavily. "Come, Nana, we're going," I said, gripping her arm. Though she seemed not to react to my voice, she obediently followed me through the hallway and out the front door to safety.

We emerged from the smoking apartment building onto the landing atop the four stone steps which separated us from the crowd below. Adrenaline was still rushing through my bloodstream and every second seemed precious. I had a blurred impression of Nana standing on the landing with parts of her multicolored shirt burned off in places, and I felt embarrassed for her. The eerie silence of the crowd disturbed me. It was as if we were high up on a stage and the crowd below was frozen into a different time dimension. Some of them were holding my children in their arms. They all seemed to be staring at me. No one spoke or came forward to offer help. I had expected to rush into the comforting arms of my neighbors who would be offering their assistance, but no one moved.

The sun was just beginning to rise. I noticed that Nana was shivering from the cold, but still no one in the crowd came forward. "We need blankets, we're cold!" I shouted. "Someone, anyone, help us, please!"

One person in the crowd assured us that an ambulance had been called, and another brought us blankets. A neighbor handed my little Shua back to me. Shua wanted to sit on my lap, so we both sat down on the stone steps together. It was comforting to have him there.

By that time, everyone in the apartment house was awake from the billowing black smoke and from the cries of "Fire!" There was great confusion too in the crowd in the street, for despite the smoke no one knew where the fire was actually coming from. It was still quite dark and the thick smoke had risen up from my windows onto the roof. Anyone seeing this would mistakenly believe that the whole building was on fire.

We heard frantic shouting back and forth from the

people inside the building to those gathered on the street. Yehoshua Mann was leaning out his fourth-floor window and shouting, "What should we do? Should we go onto the roof, or jump out the windows? Is it safe to come down the stairs?" The strange thought I'd had while descending the steps in darkness from the Manns' apartment that *erev Shabbat* just two weeks earlier suddenly flashed through my mind. I understood now that it had been a premonition telling me that the stairs were a safe escape route. I was also the only one who knew that the source of the fire was my apartment. I yelled back to Yehoshua with confidence, "Just come down the stairs. It's safe. Don't be afraid." In less than a minute, Yehoshua emerged, followed by Sima and their baby daughter.

I heard a young girl screaming hysterically from the third floor. People were trying to convince her to leave her apartment but she shouted back, "I'm not dressed. I'm not coming down!" I felt embarrassed for this helpless girl. She reminded me of a kitten stuck in a tree. If she were a bird she could have flown away, but as it was she was trapped. I think I yelled back up to her, "Just come down. There's no time for this — your life is at stake!" Fortunately, my message got through to her. She managed to come down, covered only by a sheet. Despite the desperation of the moment, everyone in the crowd averted their eyes as she slipped into the darkness to safety.

When everyone had gotten out of the building safely, it became very quiet. The fire was still raging and roaring in our apartment, but the residents of the building, *baruch Hashem*, were all right. Suddenly, I looked down at my left hand and saw that the skin had separated from the flesh of my thumb, and was attached only by the fingernail.

That's when I realized that my life would never be the same again. But such thoughts had no place now. We needed to get moving.

As Nana and I waited, I looked up at the crowd of

neighbors and at the smoking building and wondered
where the fire trucks and the ambulances were. Though
they had been called some time before, they apparently
could not get through the narrow Old City alleys, turn
the corners and maneuver the streets which had been
designed for chariots and donkey carts two thousand
years before. According to the accounts I later read in
the Israeli press, when the firemen finally reached their
destination, they couldn't locate the wrench with which
to open the fire hydrant or the key to the area where the
gas balloons of the building were stored. A garden hose
was supplied by one of the residents.

As I tried to stand up, Shua slid off my lap, inadvertently
causing my first sensation of pain. It was a vague scraping
feeling on my thighs. Other than that I really didn't feel
anything at all.

"Nana," I said, "let's go!" How long could we wait, I
wondered, in the shape we were in. Wrapped in blankets,
we walked away from the crowd towards the Ramban
synagogue, where I remembered the ambulance was usually parked. Having seen the condition of my hand, I
realized I would need some serious medical attention, but
I did not know the extent of the burns I had incurred. I
had no idea, as I walked away from my children, that we
would be separated for such a long time. Our goodbyes
were therefore very brief as I placed Shua into the arms of
a smiling neighbor, never doubting that he and the other
children would be well taken care of. We left as Devorah
was enjoying the slippers someone had brought her to
wear. Only later did I find out that my sister and brother-
in-law took the children to be examined by a doctor at
the local health fund clinic and they were found to be
fine, without as much as a scratch.

I've been asked how I was able to walk by myself.
Wasn't the pain unbearable? After all, I had sustained
massive, severe second- and third-degree burns covering

eighty-five percent of my body. At the time, however, I had no sensation of pain. I wasn't thinking then; I was just doing. I suppose that when one's adrenaline level is high, as mine must have been, one simply acts. But it was as if Hashem was standing right there next to me, helping me to do what needed to be done.

If you had asked me then whether I saw myself as the kind of person who had great faith, I would have answered, "No, not me. This one or that one, yes; but not me." Since then my teachers have taught me that Hashem doesn't test a person who can't stand up to the challenge. He must have given me the depth of faith I required.

Nana and I were accompanied by two of my neighbors as we staggered the 150 yards down the ancient Old City streets to the Churvah Square. One of the men had offered to drive us to the hospital in his car, but instinctively I knew I needed to lie down in an ambulance. I couldn't imagine having to sit up in a car for the drive down the long, winding road to the hospital.

As we approached the square, which was in the process of renovation, we stumbled over the stones and rubble from the destroyed structures that had surrounded it. To our relief we saw the waiting ambulance parked at the entrance of the square. As we approached it we were horrified to discover that there was no driver in sight. Rather than waiting helplessly for the ambulance to come to our aid, we had gone out with great anticipation to meet it. Instead, we found a dark and deserted ghost town — a dead end. Burnt, cold and weak, we stared at the driverless ambulance with dismay, not knowing what we should do. After several anxious moments the driver appeared as if from nowhere. He had gone out to search for us.

Because of Nana's age, I assume, the driver began to tend to her first, but Nana, understanding the situation better than he, insisted I get into the ambulance before she did. I don't know if she realized then how seriously hurt I was. I do know about the beautiful quality of selflessness that she has always possessed, always putting others' needs before her own. I wasn't consciously aware of how badly burnt I was, but the fact is I didn't protest.

I remember lying down on the ambulance cot and receiving oxygen, and I was vaguely conscious of the driver getting Nana settled in the other cot. It was still dark outside, and as I closed my tired eyes I felt a tremendous wave of relief just to be there. My mind was letting go. I had collapsed. It was time to finally give up being in charge: my children were safe and so was Nana; the neighbors too were out of the burning building — that job was done. I still felt no physical pain. The only feeling I had was the anticipation of arriving at the hospital and being taken care of.

In *Pirkei Avot*, it is written: "Ben Zoma says, Who is strong? He who subdues his personal inclination, as it is said: 'He who is slow to anger is better than the strong man, and a master of his passions is better than a conqueror of a city.'" I had heard of the Rabbi who saw soldiers returning from battle and said to them: "You think you've had a long and difficult struggle. You made it home safely. But look out for the real battle now, the battle against the *Yetzer Ha-Ra*, the Evil Inclination." Up until then my battle had been physical, one of bringing everyone out of the fire safely. Now my spiritual battle had begun. The doctors would help me fight my physical battle, but I would have to fight the spiritual one alone. My weapons would be my prayers and the belief that Hashem would always be there for me.

We were driven to the emergency entrance of Hadassah Hospital on Mount Scopus. The ambulance driver, apparently wanting to get us to the closest hospital, had chosen Mount Scopus, never imagining they would be unable to treat us there. After discerning the extent of our burns, the emergency room doctors understood immediately that we needed to be treated at the special Burns Unit of Hadassah Ein Kerem, at the other end of the city. Thus we were sent back in the direction we had come, to Hadassah Hospital in Ein Kerem, many more kilometers of endless, winding roads away. At about 6:30 A.M., we finally reached our destination.

I was so relieved to at last be in the right hospital that nothing else bothered me. I lay there covered with a green army blanket, waiting for a doctor to come, feeling vaguely that I had been there before. Suddenly I realized why the room looked familiar.

It was in fact only weeks before, under somewhat different circumstances, that I had been in this very room. Simcha had left early that morning to drive to Tel Aviv for the day. Shua, being an active two-and-a-half-year-old, was running up and down the hallway of our new apartment, when suddenly I heard a loud scream. My little boy was standing in the doorway with blood streaming down his face. My heart leaped into my throat. I looked more closely and saw that he had a deep gash over his eye. My mind raced as I tried to figure out what to do. With Simcha away, it was up to me. As we had lived in this neighborhood only two weeks, I didn't know what procedure I should follow, so I quickly called my neighbor Yehoshua on the phone. "Shua is bleeding," I told him. "We need to go to the hospital *now*. What's the fastest way — ambulance, taxi, car?" Yehoshua decided that calling an ambulance was the best thing to do. I soon learned that this meant running out to meet the ambulance in the parking lot.

My neighbor offered to carry Shua for me but my little boy became hysterical, kicking and screaming for his *Imma*. I hoisted him up and carried him all the way to the end of Chabad Street. He was heavy but he calmed down in my arms. It seemed to take a very long time until the ambulance finally arrived. As we stood there waiting and waiting, Yehoshua and I agreed that it might have been better to call a taxi. When the ambulance came at last, we quickly jumped in and sped off to the emergency room.

The long drive to Hadassah Ein Kerem was exhausting for me, as I tried to keep little Shua calm and apply enough pressure on his deep wound to stanch the bleeding. As soon as we reached the hospital the medic took him to the emergency operating room. They sedated him immediately and began the operating procedure. He was covered with a white sterile cloth in which a hole was left open surrounding the gash above his eye. After cleaning the wound, the surgeon began to stitch it, when suddenly Shua woke up. He was terrified. Finding himself under a sheet, he started kicking and screaming for his mother. The surgeon moved the hole in the cloth over slightly so that Shua could see me. The sight of his wound, his eye peering up at me, the blood, the long needle, made me queasy. I felt my knees growing weak. "I feel faint," I said, and collapsed into a nurse's arms. The moment I awoke in this same emergency room, on a bed much like the one I was now lying on, I saw my friend Leah, who had just arrived. She was holding Shua's hand, and he was toddling along the corridor beside her, clutching the string of his "balloon" — an inflated surgical glove the staff had provided. It was a comforting and heartwarming sight to see his long blonde banana curls bouncing under the little *kippah* on his head and his neatly bandaged brow. It was as if nothing had happened. All the excitement was over.

The cords of death encircled me... I found
trouble and sorrow.
Then I called upon the Name of Hashem:
Please, Hashem, save my soul!
Gracious is Hashem, and righteous;
our God is merciful.

TEHILLIM 116:3-5

 I AWOKE FROM this dream-like memory to see my father-in-law Sam leaning over me, whispering in my ear. My in-laws, great lovers of Israel, were accustomed to spending several months each year visiting here. This time they were accompanied by Simcha's twin brothers David and Jonathan. It was fortunate that they all just happened to be in Israel at the time that the fire broke out and when I needed them the most.

Sam didn't want to disturb my thoughts or cause me to strain myself. I can't remember exactly what he said to me, but I know they were words of care and concern. My father-in-law was the first person to ask me how I was feeling, and what had happened. Neither my neighbors, nor the ambulance attendant, nor any doctor or nurse had asked me. All along there had been no personal interaction. I had felt very alone. What a relief it was to speak to him. I began to feel taken care of.

I gave Sam a brief synopsis of the events. He was totally accepting. Some people have asked why I didn't jump out the window or run out the door. He never pressed me about what I did or didn't do. He just reassured me that he'd personally make sure that I'd have the best doctors and get the best care possible. With my husband away, my father-in-law took complete responsibility for me. In fact my in-laws had always been there for us, since the beginning of our marriage. Sam had this quality of moving in where there was a need to be filled. Over the years we have discovered the great extent of his acts of *chesed* for people outside our immediate family. Orphans, widows, penniless new immigrants in need, depended on his emotional and physical support. *Baruch Hashem*, he was there to help me now.

I remember the nurses calling for blue sheets, which I later learned meant sterile sheets. Then my trials began. One nurse came over and gently helped me to sit up and remove my robe, which had already begun to adhere to my open wounds. Each piece of clothing that I wore had protected the skin underneath it. My turtleneck shirt completely protected my neck, and the ankle-high quilted slippers that Nana had brought me on her visit had left my feet unscathed. Even my watch protected the skin underneath: to this day its shape remains imprinted on my wrist as a witness.

The nurse was explaining that when a person suffers burns as severe as mine, only non-dyed, white cotton cloth must be used to cover the wounds. Because my hands had already swelled up, it was excruciatingly painful when she pulled off my wedding ring. I remember how amazed she was to discover that my cotton headscarf had not even been singed, and had so miraculously escaped the flames that I had run through. As a married Orthodox woman, I had always worn a scarf to cover my hair.

Then the nurses placed me gently down on the bed and covered me with a sterile blue sheet. I saw that my grandmother was lying on the bed next to mine. When my sister Miriam arrived, she must have thought I was sleeping. "Nana," I heard her whisper. "I called Mom and Dad, and they're coming as soon as they can get a ticket. We have to be strong, Nana. The doctors are doing everything they can for you and Malka." She paused. "It might take a long time."

Suddenly I understood that there was a chance that I might die! I had never contemplated dying. Thoughts began to race through my mind. I had only recently heard of the sudden death of a young mother of small children — like me! — whose husband had subsequently married a friend of mine, a religious woman of fine character. The idea that this could be happening to me came as a shock. One moment I was young and healthy and thought nothing could possibly happen to me and then suddenly the idea that my own life could be cut short had become a reality.

I had learned how Moshe *Rabbenu* pleaded with Hashem for his life to be extended so that he could enter Eretz Yisrael. He who was the greatest defender of *Am Yisrael* had to defend himself. I decided then and there that with every bit of energy I had, I would fight for my life. "Please, Hashem," I began to pray silently, "let me live! Let me finish the job you gave me! I want to be a wife to my husband and a mother to my children!" Every other relationship faded at that moment.

❋   ❋   ❋

For three difficult days nothing else mattered. All other aspirations and desires that I had in life drifted far away into the background — temporarily forgotten. Things had become crystal-clear to me: This was what I had been created for. There was no conflict or struggle in me — it just came forward. Life was the only thing worth fighting for. My relationship with Hashem grew very intense.

I was heavily sedated with morphine and had no sensation in my body. The only pain I felt during those three days was from the tube that was put down my throat to help me breathe. The doctors were concerned about the damage to my lungs caused by smoke inhalation.

Professor Menachem Ron Wexler, head of Hadassah's Department of Plastic and Maxillofacial Surgery, directed the medical team which cared for me. Months after the fire, he told my husband that in burn cases like mine, he never knew, when he finished his work in the hospital at night, if he would see his patients again in the morning. "Many years ago," he said, "severely burned patients often died of shock during the first few days. Then we learned how to nurse patients safely through the shock period. Still, until recently, all that achieved was to postpone death for a little while. Patients who survived the shock period would succumb to infection two weeks later.

"Luckily for your wife, we've discovered that with super aggressive treatment, excising the infected dead tissue through surgery, and covering those areas with skin grafts, we can save patients once doomed to death."

After the ordeal of the first three days, I was still alive. At that point I believed strongly that I would live.

I didn't know that the doctors had told my family that I would have, at best, a one in ten chance for survival. Yet during the six weeks that I was on the critical list, neither the doctors, nor my parents who had arrived immediately from the U.S. to be at my side, nor my husband or any other friend or member of my family ever presented a picture of anything but positive encouragement and support.

I remember my brother-in-law David, coming to see me while I was still in the emergency room. He looked calm and not alarmed at my appearance, which prompted me to ask if he recognized me. "Yeah, sure," he said. "You look like you have a bad sunburn." His words consoled me and I thought I could imagine how I looked, because once before I'd fallen asleep under a sun lamp and the burn caused my whole face to swell.

Since I was so heavily sedated, only my face felt slightly swollen. During those three days, I was totally inside myself, not relating to my physical being, my tactile sensations. Months later, I remember thinking: Here I am, the same person inside but my body is completely different from what it was before the fire. What was left of my burnt and blackened skin was exposed, sometimes turning green from infection; my hands were distorted and purple, swollen to two or three times their normal size, and some of their bones were fused. I remember asking myself, What is a woman? The clothes she wears, her beautiful face, her position in society? *Baruch Hashem*, within myself, deep down inside my thoughts and feelings, I felt no different from the person I had been the day before the fire.

Before I became religious, I wanted to be a famous artist. I felt that when I was older I would be able to give expression to a noteworthy cause, a unique message. I had always been known as someone with "golden hands." Ironically, my hands were the most badly burnt part of my body, but that didn't matter to me now. It was as if Hashem had imprisoned me in this damaged body and the sentence I had to endure was the pain of my recovery. I thought of Yaakov, who for seven years labored for Lavan, his future father-in-law, in order to win the hand of his beloved Rachel (*Bereshit* 29), and I strengthened my resolve to take each day on its own merit, with Hashem's help, in order to reach my goal — getting well — so that I would one day function as a healthy wife and mother again. Being so close to death, I saw clearly that this was the essence of life.

I never lost consciousness — not during the explosion, nor during the long ride in the ambulance, nor in the hospital emergency room. But the moment of feeling completely awake came as I opened my swollen eyes to see my husband standing beside my bed.

Simcha had rushed home from New York less than twenty-four hours after his arrival there. He and his friend

Avraham Rosenblum, leader of the Diaspora Yeshiva Band, had arrived in the States on Tuesday. They were staying in Simcha's parents' apartment in New York while my in-laws were visiting Israel. After a busy day of running around getting ready for their U.S. tour, they fell soundly asleep early that night. It must have been about two o'clock in the morning when the shrill ringing of the telephone jolted them awake.

Rabbi Goldstein was on the phone from Jerusalem. "There's been a bad fire in your house," he told Simcha, sounding very distraught. "Your children are fine, but your wife was injured. Come back right away." A few minutes later his parents called from Israel with the same message. Luckily, Simcha was not alone. Avraham was with him, and they waited as the hours passed until it was time to attend the early morning prayer services in the local synagogue. Simcha called my parents in Connecticut, and as soon as the working day started, he and Avraham rushed to the travel agent on the Lower East Side to purchase a return ticket to Israel.

It was late Thursday night when Simcha arrived at Ben Gurion Airport. His brothers and parents were waiting for him, and they all burst into tears as they embraced. As they drove from the airport to Jerusalem, his brother Jonathan, an oncologist at a well-known New York Hospital, explained to Simcha exactly what my condition was, preparing him for the worst. Until then, the critical nature of the situation had not sunk in.

❄   ❄   ❄

As Simcha entered the Intensive Care Unit at Hadassah, with its machines beeping and blinking, the staff speaking in low, hushed tones behind him, he felt very frightened. Struggling to control his emotions, he braced himself as he approached the door of my isolation chamber. "Keep calm," he told himself as he reached for the knob. "You don't want to upset her any more than she is already." And then he saw me, raised up on a very high bed, wrapped in white gauze like a mummy. His eyes filled with tears. That was the moment I opened my eyes and saw him standing there.

"I love you, Malka! Hashem will help us. Our prayers will help us," was all he could say. We both burst into tears. It must have been terrible for him as it was for me. The doctors insisted he leave then. They were afraid to let him spend more than a minute with me, hovering as I was between life and death. This was the first time they had seen me cry and felt that I could not stand any further strain.

Simcha went straight to Mount Zion to see our Rabbi. When Rabbi Goldstein saw him, he cried out emotionally, "Ah, Simcha! You have suffered a hard blow. Your beloved wife! Your home! All your possessions! The Rambam tells us that when trouble comes to a person, he must realize that it is from Hashem, and do *teshuvah* immediately." Our Rabbi knew that Simcha had to grab the moment and cry out to Hashem. He instructed Simcha to organize a *minyan*, right then and there, to recite the entire book of *Tehillim* — all one hundred and fifty psalms — in King David's Tomb. At that point he also added "Chaya" to my name, from the Hebrew root meaning "life."

Simcha's back was turned to the men who were praying with him. He told me afterwards that he thought he heard thousands of voices weeping behind him as he began to read the opening verses of King David's *Tehillim.* Each verse was sung out loud, and one after another evoked tears, moans, and cries from the tightly packed crowd in the reverberating cave-like room. For three solid hours of intense concentration, their voices rose up to Heaven in a rising crescendo of emotion. Together with King David, they sang songs of Praise.

> The right hand of Hashem is exalted, the right hand of
> Hashem performs deeds of valor.

It seemed as if the whole world was joining them in a
song of trust, a song of praise.

> I shall not die; for I shall live and relate the deeds of
> Hashem. Hashem has chastened me exceedingly, but He
> did not let me die.

Afterwards, as Simcha tried to leave, he was unable to
walk without leaning on his friends. He had been totally
drained of all his physical and emotional strength.

Later in the day, Simcha and his friends decided to
return to the burnt apartment to see if there was anything
salvageable. "I touched the walls," Simcha told me dazedly,
"and they were still hot, cracked, and black..." A smokey
haze had filled the whole house. It was like being inside
an oven, even though twenty-four hours had passed since
the fire had broken out. The stench of burnt plastic was
everywhere. "Everything is still there," Simcha reported.
"I looked at the fridge — the body is intact but the door
melted into a blob of hardened plastic. Like the tape
recorder. The little room next to the kitchen where you
kept your sewing things, Malka, was burnt to a crisp. The
children's room is fine." Later, Simcha told me that when
he looked into our bedroom he saw that our mattresses
had been left untouched by the fire except for a longish
burnt slash in the middle of my bed — my image. "Seeing
that shook me," he said. "I can't find any other word.
Somehow I found the strength to leave."

❋   ❋   ❋

The next day I underwent the first of my nine skin-
graft operations. Simcha stood outside the operating room
door, crying.

Inside the operating theater, and under anesthesia, I was engulfed by warmth and love. In a large angelic choir I sang solo. Every part of me echoed my song: *I love you Hashem. I love you. I love you.*

When I awoke, I was sure I had really been singing out loud. Surely I had disturbed the operating team in their work! What did they think of me? "How silly," they must have said to each other. "Why is she singing like that?" I felt embarrassed at the thought that they had seen a glimpse of my innermost self. But no reference of any kind was made to my singing, by the doctors or any of the nurses. Perhaps the singing of the soul is not audible in this world.

That afternoon a friend came to visit me in the recovery room. She told Simcha and me that my eyes looked extraordinary, like eyes that had seen prophecy.

After about a week of heavy morphine sedation, the doctor decided to put me on other painkillers, to avoid morphine addiction. Unfortunately, such painkillers were inferior to morphine in effectiveness and that meant that, even while medicated, I was in pain now. Any little movement of a muscle or limb was excruciating. I remember how I had to prepare myself for the painful procedure of having the sheets of my bed changed. First I had to roll over to one side. After the nurses pushed the used sheet next to me and replaced it with a clean one, I had to roll back over both of them so that the clean one could be tucked in on that side. The pain of moving and having pressure on my skin was so excruciating that the only way I could get myself to move when I had to, was by giving myself orders. "Okay, here goes," I would tell myself authoritatively. "It's just going to take a second. Take a deep breath. Roll!" Then I'd have to experience the pain all over again when I rolled back. And when they finished making the bed, I had to maneuver myself back to the middle. Intense pain — sometimes unbearable — became part of my daily life.

The ten percent chance of survival given me by the doctors would be valid for six weeks. The body's protective covering of skin helps regulate temperature, retains vital fluids, and is sensitive to tactile sensations, including pain. It also protects the body against bacteria. With only fifteen percent of my skin undamaged, covering my charred body, and with my lungs possibly severely damaged from smoke inhalation, my chances of recovery were close to impossible.

Bless Hashem, O my soul, and forget not
all His favors… Who heals all your illnesses,
Who redeems your life from destruction,
Who encircles you with love and compassion.

TEHILLIM 103:2-4

AFTER ABOUT A WEEK in the Intensive Care Unit, I was transferred to the Burn Unit on the seventh floor where I spent the next three-and-a-half months. Sam and Simcha's brother, Doctor Jonathan, concerned about my care, approached the Director of the Burn Unit, Professor Wexler, and asked him if he would take me as his private patient. Professor Wexler relieved their worries by telling them that it was not necessary. I would be getting the best possible medical care, and the cost would be covered by our health insurance. "I will be available for Chaya Malka all the time," he reassured them. "After all, my office is right here, and — fortunately — we're not that busy now." Even though he loved his work, this caring physician felt fortunate when "business was slow" and there were no other burn victims to tend to. I see this as one of the many kindnesses from Above — that my accident took place at a time when the hospital ward was still empty. In another six months the war in Lebanon would begin and the ward would be filled to capacity with our injured soldiers.

Since I was the only critical case there at the time, I was the prima donna of the ward. The nurses and doctors

cared for me around the clock. At the beginning I spent
time watching blinking digital numbers on the two big
machines to which I was hooked up. The sheets were
still blue, the room itself was sterile, and whoever came
to see me had to wear a sterilized robe and a surgical
mask. Actually I had all kinds of visitors. Trying to solve
the mystery of my constantly recurring high fevers, my
doctor would periodically bring experts into my room;
once a heart specialist, another time a liver specialist. All
of a sudden there would be a great flurry of activity. The
doctors would all march into my room, bombard me with
lots of questions, study my charts, check my blood test
results, and recheck the numbers, trying to find some sort
of clue about what was causing these high fevers.

❄   ❄   ❄

My husband's arrival was much awaited this night
for it was the first night of Chanukah. After Simcha lit
candles at home with the kids and our parents, he would
come to the hospital to light for me. There was much
debate as to whether or not the lighting inside my sterile
environment would be a threat to my health. Finally
it was decided that Simcha would light behind the glass
partition separating my room from the nurse's station. The
hospital staff gathered around as Simcha lit our menorah
on the partition shelf. I watched through the glass. All
eyes focused on the menorah as the mesmerizing flame
simultaneously set their faces aglow. How beautiful and
unthreatening a flame could look in this form, I thought.
Thanking Hashem for the miracle of Chanukah, we prayed
for our own miracle, one that would allow us to continue
our lives together.

❄   ❄   ❄

Simcha moved back to Mount Zion with our two oldest
children, Devorah and Shua. He was greatly relieved when

Rabbi Goldstein offered him a small apartment there that his late father had lived in. Our baby, Esther, would be living in the Jewish Quarter with some close friends from the Yeshiva. Simcha was grateful to be surrounded by the warmth and supportive atmosphere of our Diaspora Yeshiva — the apartment was in the complex of Yeshiva housing. Our old apartment over King David's Tomb had been boarded up by the municipality.

Our neighbors arranged to have food prepared for the family on a regular basis. A few years before, a program was instituted at the Yeshiva, which we called "Meals for Mothers and Others." All the families in the community participated. We would all sign up, each woman for a different day, to provide a hot meal every day for three weeks for a woman and her family after childbirth. This would enable the new mother to gain back her strength. If people were ill, they would also receive meals. This *chesed* program has been an important part of our community ever since.

People were constantly asking if they could help in other ways as well. Simcha was being bombarded by so many different emotions at the time, having to cope with my life-threatening situation, with seeing me in such pain, with the physical care of the children, and with the children's emotions, that he felt he could not respond personally to all the inquiries about my condition and all the offers of help. At one point he even felt he just wanted to be left alone, although he appreciated people's desires to help. It was decided then that all questions concerning my condition, as well as all offers of assistance, would go through my friend Leah. She became the official spokeswoman for the hospital and our family.

Sometimes Simcha felt uncomfortable being the recipient of so much help from our community. "You know," he told me, "we come from a society where a person, especially a man, must be tough and strong...able to fend for himself, to pick himself up by his bootstraps, so to speak. But ever since we started learning Torah, Malka, we've had to change our values. The Chafetz Chayim says, on *Sefer Tehillim*, that the world is built on lovingkindness and that kindness is the energy that rotates the wheels of existence. After eating or drinking, a Jew praises Hashem with the blessing 'Who creates numerous living things with their deficiencies,'" Simcha went on. "Hashem created man with deficiencies and shortcomings so that others would be compelled to help him overcome those deficiencies. Whatever one is missing, the other makes up. As a result, through both sides, the world continues to exist. It's been difficult to accept all our friends' offers of help, Malka, even though I couldn't do without it. A Jew is emulating the ways of Hashem, the Merciful King, when he takes from his own and gives to others. And at the same time," Simcha concluded, "he also recognizes his own needs and those of his family and is able to let others extend a helping hand."

Chesed came in many forms. Just as it was important to help the running of our household, it was also essential that people remember us in their prayers. I didn't know then, nor did Simcha, what an effect our tragedy had on other people's lives. "Life stopped for all of us," people told him. For six weeks people were in shock. He met someone at the Western Wall, someone we didn't even know, who had been praying for us for days with the intensity of someone praying for a member of his own family.

* * *

The Burn Unit at Hadassah Ein Kerem was quite small. It consisted of three main rooms and a nurses' station. The first room — where I spent three-and-a-half months — had two vital-signs machines and a glass partition window, so that my bed was directly visible from the nurses' station across the way. Further down the hall from the nurses' station was a room for less severe cases. The third room — where I spent my last month in the hospital — was called the "going home room." It was more friendly, with its own shower and private bathroom. There was also a glass partition window facing the hallway so the staff could check on patients without disturbing them. There were other rooms for plastic surgery, medical staff meetings, and a waiting room for visiting guests.

A room with a kidney-shaped bath was also part of the Burn Unit. Every day, twice a day, I was taken into the room where the bath was. Every second in the room itself consisted of either anticipating pain or experiencing tremendous pain. One of the nurses would come into my room beforehand, take my arm, and give me a combined shot of Valium and painkiller. A few minutes after she left, I would start to feel relaxed, then euphoric, and then sleepy. Ten minutes later two nurses would come back into the room and lift me onto a special stretcher placed on top of a bed on wheels. As the bed was rolled through the hallway, with each turn I was gripped with fear of what I was about to experience. Each step of the procedure was part of the long, drawn-out dreaded torture. The nurses rolled me in, clipped the stretcher onto a crane by the four hooks on the corners of my portable bed, and lifted me up until I was suspended in midair. I felt like a load of bricks dangling from a crane over a construction site. Then they slowly lowered me, on my stretcher, into the bath. There was a huge heater suspended from the ceiling hanging over me. It was the biggest heater I'd ever seen. In my worst moments, the feeling of a little warmth coming from that heater was the only physical comfort I ever had.

The bath was as large as a small swimming pool. The nurses would lean over me in the water and slowly begin to unravel my white gauze bandages, limb by limb, joint by joint. The feeling of having these bandages removed was like having my skin ripped off. Sometimes after the bandages had been taken off, the nurses would scrub my raw flesh. "Removing the burnt skin is a painful and time-consuming job, but it is absolutely necessary," Dr. Wexler had explained to me. "The greater the extent of the burn, the greater the chance of infection."

Sometimes a physiotherapist would come to exercise my body in the water, where it was less agonizing. Then I was put back on the mobile stretcher, the bandages were soaked in sterile saline solution, and the nurse began slowly to wrap me up again, limb after limb, each digit, each joint, until I was wrapped like an Egyptian mummy. Then they wheeled me back to my room.

That's when I would begin to shiver. The huge heater had warmed me in the bath and I now started to feel cold. This happened every single time. The feeling of cold slowly intensified so that by the time I had been wheeled back to my room I was shivering intensely. Oddly enough, I never dreaded the shivering because the pain of the bath which preceded it was so much worse. Nevertheless, it drained me of the little energy that I had. It usually lasted about two hours, and felt like it would never end. I was out of control then; there was no stopping it. It was the same every day. I couldn't speak to Simcha when he'd come to visit me at these times.

It took a little while for me to understand the delicate balance of my situation in which one extra blanket would cause my fever to go up. I had come to recognize, some-times better than the nurses, this balance, and tried to warn them of the impending danger but some didn't listen to me. I had already been through it so many times, that it was hard trying to convince them in my shivering state to cover me with only one blanket, especially after seeing the incredible soothing warmth that the blankets gave me.

They would insist that it was all right, wanting to comfort me, but then the fever would begin to rise within half an hour after I had been covered with so many blankets, and they'd have to take them all off, leaving one thin sheet to cover me, and sprinkle water on the sheet. The nurse would turn on a fan, and have it blow cool air on me to bring the fever down. It was hours of this, back and forth — the bath, the shivering, the blankets, the fever, the fan, being hot, being cold.

One day I overheard Professor Wexler instructing the nurse to have my bandages changed four times that day. This felt like too much to endure. Though I knew it would help me, I was only human, and I dreaded the baths. *Baruch Hashem*, that day they changed the bandages only three times.

Nana, who'd suffered burns over thirty-five percent of her body, was undergoing treatment too. She was moved to another floor so that she would be spared having to hear her granddaughter's screams.

Once as I was lying in the bath, exhausted and weak, after all the bandages had been taken off, several doctors came into the room to examine me. I was overcome with embarrassment and helplessness, so exposed and there was nothing I could do. Another time when I was in the bath, after they had stopped giving me morphine and I was only on Valium, I screamed from the pain, insisting I couldn't endure it anymore, begging to be given a strong painkiller. The doctors put some solution into the intravenous drip, which I am convinced to this day was nothing more than a placebo, because my pain didn't subside at all. Later, I figured out that Valium was a drug which gave me a false sense of relief but did not lessen the pain. They stopped giving me Valium on my own request and I went to the bath with no painkiller at all. Specialists were called in to teach me self-hypnosis. It was exciting to think I'd be learning this technique, but I fell asleep during each lesson.

I had always thought that nurses were nurturing and loving women whose task was to make the sick feel better, giving medicine and treatment with gentleness. Some nurses in the hospital were angelic, always sweetly reassuring me and soothing my emotions with smiling faces. To my shock and dismay, though, many of the nurses seemed to me more like the attendants of Gehinnom in my torture chamber, causing me excruciating pain.

Whenever I saw the cold hard face of a certain demanding nurse, I felt dread. And yet, by the prodding insistence which seemed so cruel at the time, I came to understand that I was capable of enduring the pain of my treatments. I began to see that she and all the nurses were messengers speeding my recovery by showing me that I could do much for myself. It didn't take long to realize how it takes a very special person with a lot of stamina to work in the Burn Unit; that it was the sweet nurses who soothed my soul, and the hard, seemingly unsympathetic ones who did their jobs efficiently but took great care not to get emotionally involved, who actually helped me face the painful treatment which was necessary for my physical recovery.

At first, Simcha used to come to the hospital in the mornings, but when he heard me screaming during a treatment in the bath, it was so devastating for him that he avoided coming in the mornings. He said it was a blood-curdling scream, like someone being murdered. The afternoons were also hard for Simcha, though, as I lay shivering with fever and covered with wet sheets. Sensing his worry and deep concern, the nurses would try to relieve the tension by joking with him about innovative ways to bring my fever down. Simcha especially liked to talk to the male nurse on night duty who, during the long winter evenings he spent in the hospital, taught him all about the details of burns and their treatments. It was

important for Simcha to have someone who was willing
to spend time with him in this way.

* * *

In the early weeks when I was on the critical list,
Simcha went to Bnei Brak to see the Steipler Rav, זצ״ל,
for a blessing. Rabbi Yasha Yisrael Kanievsky was one of
the greatest Rabbis of our time, a brilliant scholar and a
righteous person. He spent the day learning Torah in his
home, and then during certain hours, he would hear the
requests of the numerous people waiting outside his door.
Thousands would flock to his home for help and advice.
It is traditional that in times of trouble the *tzaddik* seeks
to subvert evil decrees through the power of his prayers.
The principle, "A *tzaddik* decrees and Hashem fulfills" has
been demonstrated throughout Jewish history.

Simcha brought an appeal which would subsequently
appear in Jewish newspapers all over Israel, Europe, and
America. It would be a way for us to raise money to
reestablish our home. It had been cosigned by other great
Rabbis of that time.

The Steipler Rav, who in his later years had become
deaf, was handed the appeal to read and asked to give me
and my family his special blessing. As the great man read
the words on the slip of paper, he was profoundly moved.
Suddenly be began to sway back and forth, moaning
"*Oy Vey!*" and "*Oy Gevalt!*" over and over, reading and
rereading the note. He placed his hand over his eyes and
started praying out loud in Yiddish with great intensity.
He reassured Simcha that he would continue to pray for
me, and gave us his blessing.

I hadn't noticed that the visitors were coming in a slow
and deliberate way. I didn't realize at the time that there
was an organized effort to control the steady stream of
visitors, so as not to drain my energy during those difficult
months in the hospital.

Urgent Plea for Help

We call upon the community to aid the family of a *ben Torah* which was struck by a terrible fire on the fourth of Kislev this year (December 2, 1981) in their apartment in the Jewish Quarter of the Old City of Jerusalem.

The mother was seriously burnt, as she saved the lives of her three children from the flames, and is now hanging on to life in the Burn Unit at Hadassah Ein Kerem. The family's belongings were destroyed and their rented apartment so badly damaged that it is no longer habitable. The family has been left with no home, and it is a great mitzvah to save this family in distress.

Signed:

    Rav S. Messas, Chief Rabbi of Jerusalem

    Rav S. Z. Broide, Rosh Yeshivat Chevron

    Rav A. Y. Zeleznik, Rosh Yeshivat Etz Chayim

    Rav S. Y. Elyashiv — "I subscribe to the above appeal."

    Rav S. Z. Auerbach, Rosh Yeshivat Kol Torah

    Rav Ovadia Yosef, Ha-Rishon Le'Tziyon, Chief Rabbi of Israel — "I hereby declare that all those who aid the above mentioned family will be blessed with all the blessings of the Torah, great happiness, wealth, honor, and all goodness."

My Prayers Were Answered

The story of the fire received wide press coverage in Israel and abroad.

To Michele Abramson, the lighting of the traditional Chanukah candles celebrates more than an ancient miracle; it serves as a tangible reminder of a personal miracle of her own.

BY BARBARA SOFER

Chanukah is a season for remembering miracles. Some 2,300 years ago a small band of Jews fought a mighty empire for the right to worship in the Temple in Jerusalem. When the Temple was rededicated, only one container of uncontaminated oil was found for the light. It burned for eight days. Today Jews all over the world light Chanukah candles to commemorate that miracle.

Chanukah has special meaning for the [...] before they light their chil[...]

in bed, searing a hole in the mattress. Her nightgown had burned up, so she grabbed a robe and ran for her children. The fire hadn't reached their room.

"I knew I had to get them out, but I couldn't think of the most efficient way," she says. Joshua, 2½, was the nearest. She clutched him to her breast and ran through a clear path to the front [...] the tele[...]

The BRIDGE

RAISE MORE THAN $16,[...] FOR 'MALKA' EMERGEN[...]

By Rosemarie Slossberg, President and Bernice Saltzman, Vice-President, Connecticut Chapter

"Malka is a lovely human being, a wonderful, special person . . . She has enormous inner resources and absolutely no self-pity . . . She and husband Simcha, have a wonderful outlook and bright hopes for the future. I felt that I had known this young couple for a long time, as if they were my own."

Such are the sentiments of APAI members and children who have visited Malka Smith Abramson, age 30, in recent weeks; people who have met Malka only since she suffered extensive burns saving her three children and grandmother from a fire which gutted her apartment in the Jewish Quarter of the Old City, Jerusalem, in early December 1981.

Raise $15,000 for Malka

The warm outpouring of love and concern for Malka from nearly 500 APAI members in the U.S. and Canada has overwhelmed those of us who initiated the appeal. About $8,000 was contributed by APAI members, chapters and the national treasury. An additional $4,200 from 270 donors in Waterbury, Connecticut, Malka's home town, came from an appeal by Mort and Fran Tarr, Connecticut Chapter members and Waterbury residents. The Tarrs made their appeal through the Waterbury Jewish Federation and through the synagogue to which they and Al and Penny Smith, Malka's parents, belong. Another $1,000 was sent to Malka from an anonymous donor in Brooklyn. $6[...]

Names of contributors, by states but without amounts, will be sent to Malka, together with the notes that accompanied many contributions. The notes expressed prayers and hopes for Malka's recovery and many wrote "wish we could send more" and "thank you for calling[...]

Malka Abramson in 1977 photo.

אלה תאר פעוט, בן שנתיים וחצי, את מעשה הגבורה של העתיקה □ האם נכוותה קשות ונשקפת סכנה לחייה

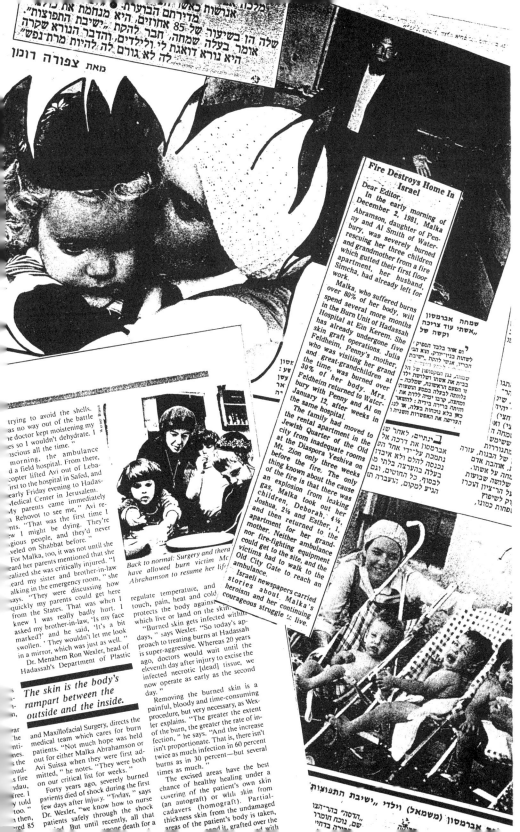

מלכה... באנשות בא... מדירתם הבוערת מנחמת את...
מדירתם הבוערת היא ישיבת התפוצות"
שלה הן בשיעור של 85 אחוזים חבר להקם שמחה בעלה לי וילדים והדבר הנורא שקרה
אומר נורא דואגת לי היא נורא גורם לה להיות מרת נפש"

מאת צפורה רוכן

Fire Destroys Home In Israel

Dear Editor:

In the early morning of December 2, 1981, Malka Abramson, daughter of Penny and Al Smith of Waterbury, was severely burned rescuing her three children and grandmother from a fire which gutted their first floor apartment, her husband, Simcha, had already left for work.

Malka, who suffered burns over 80% of her body, will spend several more months in the Burn Unit of Hadassah Hospital at Ein Kerem. She has already undergone five skin graft operations. Julia Feldheim, Penny's mother, who was visiting her grand and great-grandchildren at the time, was burned over 30% of her body. Mrs. Feldheim returned to Waterbury with Penny and Al on January 12, after weeks in the same hospital.

The family had moved to the rental apartment in the Jewish Quarter of the Old City from inadequate rooms at the Diaspora Yeshiva on Mt. Zion only three weeks before the fire. The only thing known about the cause of the fire is that there was an explosion from leaking gas. Malka took out her children, Deborah, 4½, Joshua, 2½ and Esther, 1, and then returned to the apartment for her grandmother. Neither ambulance nor fire-fighting equipment could get to the site, and the victims had to walk to reach an Old City Gate to reach an ambulance.

Israeli newspapers carried stories about Malka's heroism and her continuing courageous struggle to live.

שמחת אברמסון "אשתי עוד צריכה וקשה של

ל... גם אחד בלבד הספיק...
לשתות בניו־יורק, הוא גני...
נלוותה, אנשי להחת, ...חביבה
חברין, ...

שמחה... גן הטטמטסוס של ילד...
זו הפם הראשוגה, שמלכה...
נלוותה לכבלוג בטם התשעות...
ומהצא, קרבה בידה ...להטבור...
היתה בברה בידה א. א...לני...
כאז בלא נתכות בעלה, א... מה...
הפרים את האפשרות השני...

בינתיים, לאחר ש...
אברמסון את דרכה אל...
נמכרה על־ידי אחד הת...
נגנבה להלם ולא אבד...
בעלה להצרצה בלהי מ...
לבסוף, כל החתום, ...
...הגיע למקום. ...

Back to normal: Surgery and thera... have allowed burn victim M... Abrahamson to resume her lif...

...trying to avoid the shells. ...as no way out of the battle ...e doctor kept moistening my ...es so I wouldn't dehydrate. I ...scious all the time. ''

...morning, the ambulance ...d a field hospital. From there, ...copter lifted Avi out of Leba...irst to the hospital in Safed, and ...early Friday evening to Hadas...Medical Center in Jerusalem. ...My parents came immediately ...n Rehovot to see me, '' Avi re...nts. "That was the first time I ...w I might be dying. They're ...igious people, and they'd never ...veled on Shabbat before. ''

...For Malka, too, it was not until she ...eard her parents mentioned that she ...ealized she was critically injured. "I ...eard my sister and brother-in-law ...alking in the emergency room, '' she ...says. "They were discussing how ...quickly my parents could get here ...from the States. That was when I ...knew I was really badly hurt. I ...asked my brother-in-law, 'Is my face ...marked?' and he said, 'It's a bit ...swollen.' They wouldn't let me look ...in a mirror, which was just as well. ''

Dr. Menahem Ron Wexler, head of Hadassah's Department of Plastic

The skin is the body's rampart between the outside and the inside.

and Maxillofacial Surgery, directs the medical team which cares for burn patients. "Not much hope was held out for either Malka Abrahamson or Avi Suissa when they were first admitted, '' he notes. "They were both on our critical list for weeks. ''

Forty years ago, severely burned patients died of shock during the first few days after injury. "Today, '' says Dr. Wexler, "we know how to nurse patients safely through the shock ...d. But until recently, all that ...one death for a

regulate temperature, and ... touch, pain, heat and cold ... protects the body against ... which live or land on the skin

"Burned skin gets infected within ... days, '' says Wexler. "So today's approach to treating burns at Hadassah is super-aggressive. Whereas 20 years ago, doctors would wait until the eleventh day after injury to excise the infected necrotic [dead] tissue, we now operate as early as the second day. ''

Removing the burned skin is a painful, bloody and time-consuming procedure, but very necessary, as Wexler explains. "The greater the extent of the burn, the greater the rate of infection, '' he says. "And the increase isn't proportionate. That is, there isn't twice as much infection in 60 percent burns as in 30 percent—but several times as much. ''

The excised areas have the best chance of healthy healing under a covering of the patient's own skin (an autograft) or with skin from cadavers (homograft). Partial-thickness skin from the undamaged areas of the patient's body is taken, ...ed it, grafted over ...with

...ar
...he
...nti-
...nes.
...s the
...nud-
...s fire
...ree. I
...too. ''
...then,
...gone 85

אברמסון (משמאל) וילדי התפוצות

הדסה בהר הצו... שם, נוכח חומר...
...קשיים בחיי"

There was a chart of time slots available for visiting hours where women would sign up. That way there would always be someone at my side to lend assistance or just to talk to.

It is said that there is no measurement for the reward for the great mitzvah of visiting the sick. I remember how our Rebbetzin gave me encouragement when she visited. It is written in the Gemara that visiting the sick takes away a percentage of their illness. When a sick person sees that everyone is concerned about his health and that others are praying for him, that in itself restores his health. Some of my friends had photographs of my children and husband framed and hung them in my hospital room. Later on they told me that they hoped these pictures would strengthen my will to live in those first critical weeks. And indeed, looking at those images of my family, in the midst of my pain, reminded me of what I was fighting for.

About a week after the fire I sent a message to Sima Mann with a friend, that I wanted very much to speak with her. I wanted to talk to someone who had actually shared those few terrifying moments back on Ararat Street. She had already sent me a tape wishing me well, and telling me how my mother-in-law had given her a gift for being so helpful and taking care of my children, the morning of the fire.

I was still completely bandaged, with only my eyes and lips exposed, when Sima came that first time. "Sima, tell me everything you remember about the fire," I said. What especially disturbed me was the replaying of the scene in my mind's eye, as I emerged from my burning apartment with my grandmother. It was shocking to me that none of my neighbors had run forward to help. I wanted to understand.

It seemed I was one of the first people to ask Sima about the fire. She hadn't talked about it yet with anyone. "It was about 5:00 A.M.," she began quietly, "and we were all sound asleep. There was an explosion which, I guess, is what woke us up. I thought it was a sonic boom, and I went back to sleep. Malka, to think you were in the middle of that explosion!" She was silent and then she began again.

"We were awakened again by loud, scary noises quickly followed by someone shouting, 'Fire! Fire!' Initially, I didn't make the connection between the cries and the explosion, because I really had gone back to sleep for at least five minutes. Suddenly I had this terrible, sinking feeling: Oh my God, It is happening. Whatever It is, that It with a capital I — war, a terrorist attack, bombing, destruction — is happening now! Because there was an urgent and eerie quality to those shouts, like someone crying out from a nightmare. At any rate, it became instantly clear that something terrible was happening, Malka. Yehoshua jumped out of bed and ran over to look out the window. 'It's a fire!' he cried.

'It can't be a fire,' I insisted. 'This is the Old City of Jerusalem, houses are made of stone, the streets of stone, the walls of stone. There's nothing to burn here, it can't be that!' Then I started to smell smoke. At that point I calmed myself down a little bit. 'Even if it's a fire,' I reassured myself, 'there's so much stone, it can't be that bad.'"

I closed my eyes, imagining how it must have been. "Go on, Sima," I whispered.

"Then we rushed to the living room, and looked out our window where we could see the beautiful skyline of the Old City and the Kotel area beyond the rooftops. Suddenly we saw flames licking the dry branches of our *sukkah* roof which was still on the balcony, and it was starting to smoke. We still didn't know how bad it was, but when we saw those flames leaping up at us, we ran back into the bedroom. Yehoshua called out the window, 'Help! Help! There's a fire!' I told him, 'Call the Fire Department, maybe no one knows about it.' He called the Fire Department and tried to explain as calmly as possible, despite his tremendous fear, the location and scope of the fire. 'Send a fire truck and an ambulance,' I remember him saying. 'The building is burning. We're on the third floor, and we don't know how bad it is.'

"Well, you know the firemen were unfamiliar with the Jewish Quarter, and they told Yehoshua to meet them by the watchman's station in the parking lot. He told them he didn't even know if he could get out of the building alive, but if he could he would meet them there as soon as possible. When he opened the front door, smoke came pouring in and we slammed the door shut. 'Let's get the keys for the door which leads up to the roof,' he said quickly. 'We'll go out the top, over to the next building and down their stairwell!'

'I don't know where the keys are,' I confessed, searching everywhere frantically — even under the bed. Part of me was very calm and at the same time I was imagining being consumed by fire. I was functioning and at the same time panicking and preparing for the worst. In the end, we didn't even try going up to the roof because I never found the keys."

"So what did you do next, Sima?"

"I remembered the films I'd seen in fifth grade during Fire Prevention Week! I took a damp towel, put it under the door and felt the doorknob to see how hot it was. Putting wet towels over our heads, we prepared to go out through the smoke. I was holding the baby at the window, putting my shoes on, because I remembered that you're supposed to put on shoes if there's a fire. Suddenly we heard a woman's voice calling up from below: 'It's safe to come down the stairs — don't be afraid.' Yehoshua opened the front door and, reassuring me he would call me if the way was clear, ran down the stairs wildly, almost flying, with a wet towel over his head. Less than a minute later I heard him calling me: 'Come down, Sima. It's okay.'

I covered myself and the baby with a wet towel, and, nervous and shaking, I left the apartment. Making my way down the hall, I knocked on a few doors. There was no response. Everyone had left already and the baby and I were the last ones out. Only about six minutes had passed since that terrible call of "Fire!" had awakened us, but it seemed like a lifetime."

How well I understood what she was describing. "And what happened when you got downstairs, Sima?"

"There were about ten people there, I think. Some were already spraying the hallway below with a garden hose. Yehoshua ran immediately to find the ambulance and direct them to the house — I guess because he had called them, he felt responsible for getting them to the fire. He told me later how, as he ran breathlessly down the street to the parking lot, he recited over and over again the Special Prayer Formula for times of trouble: the Thirteen Qualities of Mercy.

"As soon as I emerged into the fresh air I saw you, Chaya Malka. You were standing there in the dark. I couldn't see very clearly because of the darkness and the smoke outside the building. I didn't realize that you were burnt so badly. It was just that your face looked gray, and I thought I saw skin hanging down from your hand, but otherwise you seemed so normal. You were sitting wrapped in a blanket with a towel around your head. Your grandmother Nana was there, looking quite upset and I could see she had burns on her legs. 'Malka needs some ice,' I said to someone in the crowd. Then you said, 'I'm going to take Nana to meet the ambulance. Sima, please take the kids to the neighbors.' I remember seeing both of you disappear down the street.

"You seemed in control. I realized it was you who had guided us down the dark stairwell and out of the building. And you directed me calmly to take the kids as you went with your grandmother to the ambulance. You and Nana had already started walking when I turned away with the kids. You're right, no one was hovering around you...I think no one realized you were really injured...I didn't even know your apartment was on fire then. The door must have been closed when I ran by. Your kids looked okay when I took them, not even black from soot or smoke."

"Tell me what happened with the kids then."

"Someone I know on Ararat Street took me and all the kids to her house. I remember putting my baby and your Esther in the playpen there. After a while we walked to your sister's. I remember also calling your friend, Leah, early in the morning. I felt very confused and shaken, but still it had not registered that you might be badly burned. Miriam took your kids immediately to be checked for smoke inhalation and they were fine. Yehoshua told me later how the fire truck and its accompanying ambulance had arrived at the watchman's station at the same time he did. He directed them into the Jewish Quarter, but to his chagrin, by the time they'd maneuvered their way through the narrow streets to the burning apartment house, you were gone. He ran back to the ambulance, redirecting the driver to where someone told him you and your grandmother had been waiting in the parking lot. By that time you were both on your way to the hospital in the first ambulance."

Sima was quiet for a few moments and then she began again. "The next thing I remember was being at the hospital with your sister Miriam. The lobby was filled with the whole Yeshiva community who came to wait outside the doors of the emergency room. Husbands and wives with baby strollers, all of the students, and of course your family were there. The hospital staff had never seen such a turnout! I still didn't understand why everyone was so concerned because you'd seemed fine when I saw you last. A social worker named Barbara was explaining to different groups of people how serious your condition was. It was then that I heard you were in critical condition." Sima was silent again. "You know, I haven't talked about this with anybody, Malka. It's been hard being with the baby alone, in our apartment, thinking about what happened. In the evenings I feel very nervous because the smell of the fire is still there. It was really scary going into your apartment, standing there the next day looking at the charred and blackened walls, and remembering being there in your house the night before, and thinking of you there."

Suddenly the mood lightened. "Do you remember how often I came to visit you during those first two weeks after you moved in, and how you and your family came for a meal on Shabbos?" she asked.

The shared memories of normal events in our recent life together was important to us both at that moment. "Of course I remember, Sima!" I tried to smile, remembering those happy days. "Do you remember two years ago when Simcha went to the States, and you stayed with me? That was before Esther was born."

"Yes," Sima answered happily, "and your grandmother stayed with us too when she came for a visit. I felt like I got to know her then. I was a single student and I used to love coming to stay with you and helping with the kids. I learned a lot about taking care of a house and children from you and Nana. Would you like me to give you a foot massage?" she suddenly asked. "I'm very good at it."

"What a great idea!" My feet had been protected from the fire by my slippers. "They could use a soothing massage," I said, and then blurted out, "Sima, there is something bothering me."

"What is it?"

"It's just that I remember coming out of the burning apartment after getting the kids out, and Nana, and..."

"How do you remember it?" Sima asked.

"I had just gone through a traumatic experience, the

adrenaline was still rushing through my blood, and I expected to run into the warm arms of my neighbors, and I could imagine them saying, 'It's okay, it's all over now, we'll take care of you... Get her a blanket! Lay her down!' You know what I mean. But instead, it was strange and silent. Nobody offered to help. I had to tell *them* what to do. 'We need blankets, we're cold, we're freezing, it's winter — please help us!' I was even directing traffic — calling people to come out of the building this way and that way. And then going to wait for the ambulance, with no driver in sight. I felt...really bad." Tears started to well up. "Tell me honestly, Sima — was it really like that or is it just that I was in shock? Were people really just standing around not offering to help? It seems so hard to believe."

Sima silently finished the massage and came and sat down by my side. "I'm sorry you experienced it that way. But no, people were not uncaring. You see, it was dark, and though it's hard to believe, you really didn't look like you were in bad shape at all! No one even knew the fire had been in *your* house. Even *I* didn't realize any of this until much later. Remember, the kids were not even scratched or sooty. No one knew. No one realized."

After hearing Sima's story, I understood better what had happened. To the crowd, I hadn't looked badly burned. They hadn't seen me on fire and in fact, I was directing people. Apparently they didn't even know where the source of the fire was. All I knew was that I needed help badly and I assumed everyone else also understood the urgency of the situation. I realized then that I should have given them the benefit of the doubt. Suddenly I felt an overwhelming exhaustion. I just had to sleep. I told Sima, and, understandingly, she left.

❄   ❄   ❄

Miriam was concerned about how I would react to seeing my face unbandaged for the first time. There was one male nurse who used to tell me how beautiful my eyes were as they peered out from the wells made by layers of white gauze that wrapped my entire face. I figured he was just trying to be nice, to make me feel positive about my appearance before I'd actually see my face in the mirror, the image that would be reflected from now on.

The day came, and I really wasn't so nervous. Looking in the mirror would be a very private moment in an atmosphere that was calm and loving. When Miriam brought me a mirror, I wasn't scared, for she took great care to prepare me for this event, to cause me the least shock possible. I had never seen alarm or panic in Miriam's eyes when she saw my face unbandaged before.

When I finally saw my reflection, the face that looked back at me was not so bad — in fact, quite nice! "I can live with this," I reassured Miriam. My face was a little swollen, but not scarred. How the burns would affect that face in the months and years to come no one could foretell. I would take one step at a time. Simcha had told me, "Beauty is skin deep, Chaya Malka. If a man marries a woman only because of her beautiful face, if her skin is burned his love too is gone. But our love is deeper — it doesn't depend on anything but itself." Then he quoted *Pirkei Avot* 5:19 to me:

> Any love which is dependent on a specific thing, when that thing is gone, the love is gone; but if is not dependent on a specific thing, it will never cease. What sort of love is dependent on a specific thing? The love of Amnon and Tamar. And which was not dependent upon a specific thing? The love of David and Jonathan.

People were shocked by my appearance. They assumed they would find a broken and downhearted woman whose face had been disfigured by the flames she had run through to save her family. When they saw me looking so much better than what they imagined, they wrongly assumed I must have undergone plastic surgery. Even though one side of my face was slightly disfigured by my burns, there was discernible physical improvement as time went by.

I explained to them that my love of Torah kept me from sorrow and despair — and that also helps to improve one's appearance. The Gemara says, in the name of R. Yehudah ben Chiya: Come and see how the ways of men are not like that of Hashem. When a man administers a medication to his fellowman, it may be beneficial to one part of the body but harmful to another. With God it is not so. He gave the Torah to Israel, and it is an elixir of life for the whole body, as it is said, "and healing to all his flesh" (*Eruvin* 54a).

Simcha was a dedicated husband who took care of all my needs. His visits were the highlight of my day. When he shared his Torah learning with me at my bedside, it was soothing and inspiring. I felt elated by his words of Torah and while he was speaking, it was as if nothing else in the world mattered.

In the Women's Division of the Yeshiva during those early years, whenever I was given the choice of studying Hebrew or studying Torah, I chose the latter. Thus when Simcha spoke, my thirst for Torah was quenched.

About a month after the fire, my children were able to visit me for the first time. I had waited with great trepidation for this moment. It had been so long since I'd seen them that I wanted to hug and kiss them immediately and yet I was physically unable to because of the pain. What could I do instead to express my love? *Baruch Hashem,* I could still give them a little smile, a twinkle of the eye, and a few gentle words. I didn't want the initial meeting to be awkward even though I was sure it would be. The nurses and the doctor were all involved in what would be best for me, best for my husband, best for my children. Since my body was always wrapped in white gauze after the baths, it was decided to schedule the visit before it was time to bandage my face. They also concluded it would be best for my children to see me sitting up in a chair.

Simcha had prepared the children for this first meeting as well as he could. "Imma has a lot of bandages," he told them gently. "She can't hug you, and you can't touch her." I couldn't imagine how I'd be able to get into a chair with all my pain. On the scheduled day, a troop of male and female nurses suddenly piled into my room as if they'd been sent on a mission. Surrounding my bed, they grabbed the corners of the sheet I was lying on, and at the count of three, despite my incredulous outcries, I was hoisted up and set down on the chair! It happened so fast, there was no time for panic. I found myself actually sitting up for the first time, which was exciting although it was very uncomfortable. They placed my arms, which were in half-casts from the elbows down, on the pillowed armrests of the chair. I tried to find a position I could feel at ease in, knowing my children would soon be there to see me. If I looked comfortable, I felt they would feel comfortable too.

The moment arrived. As my husband and children walked into my room, my eyes filled with tears. Esther had just started to walk, and she was still a chubby little baby doll with her clear blue eyes. Shua, with his angelic face and long curls bouncing as he walked, was still a happy-go-lucky little boy. (My father-in-law called him "two-by-two" because he was so solidly built.) Devorah's beautiful face still shone like sunshine and she was the same very active skinny little girl. It seems it was only Simcha and I who were nervous. Little children aren't nervous — it is just not their reality. As they walked in — or rather bounced in — I melted. How I had missed the joy of watching them grow and being there for them! There I was sitting up in a chair, "a mummy with a robe on," as Simcha described it. The kids were timid at first. It is written in our sources that in the whole world there are no two voices, faces, or minds exactly alike. And when they heard me speaking, they knew I was still their *Imma*, their Mom. Although the setting was completely alien to them and although I looked so different, wrapped up and stiff, and it had been a long month, they still remembered me. I was grateful when I realized that my voice was the same as it had always been and that it helped bridge the gap between us now. I knew my heart and mind hadn't changed, but it had never occurred to me that my voice had also remained unchanged. In my anxiety about our first meeting I had overlooked this gift. I felt comforted and reassured that they were happy. We talked a bit though it was still slightly strained.

After that first visit, they came often, and their visits sustained me. Once it snowed on the afternoon that we had planned a visit. I watched expectantly by the window and my eyes impatiently scoured the white street below for some sign of my husband and children. Did the snow prevent them from coming? Suddenly I heard their sweet voices outside my door. If I could have, I would have run out to catch my precious, happy children up into my arms. With a prayer of thanks on my lips that they had come despite the snow, I welcomed them. Their bubbling voices filled my room with happiness.

❋ ❋ ❋

The skin covers the body and all its organs in a very beautiful way, and yet when it is suddenly opened — in a wound, or in surgery, or in a burn — a window is opened into a whole world that we never see. When my son gashed the skin above his eye I could hardly believe what I was looking at. How amazingly did Hashem form our bodies and cover them with the miracle of skin. In the beginning, I was operated on in order to clear away the burnt and blackened skin. Since eighty-five percent of my skin was damaged, the most important thing was to remove the dead tissue and replace it with the covering of my own undamaged skin, or skin from other sources. This was the best chance I had of healing, because new skin would serve to retain body heat and protect me from infection.

The hospital was in close contact with an institute in Tel Aviv which had cadaver and animal skin available for grafting. This resource was used in the very beginning to save my life. Later on, the skin for grafting was taken from my own body: from my head, my shoulders, and my abdomen. At first I underwent skin graft surgery every two weeks for three-and-a-half months. Later, it was at more irregular intervals; different levels of burns had different needs. Some deep third-degree burns needed more grafting, while the skin regenerated spontaneously on others.

It always seemed to me that as much skin as there was available, it could never be enough to cover the areas that needed grafts. After every operation, the areas where skin had been excised for grafting took two weeks to heal. Sometimes the itching of the healing skin became so overpowering that I couldn't sleep, and I would find myself scratching the bandages off, to the dismay of the nursing staff. Although I tried not to complain, I was in agony and exhausted, with no relief in sight.

The last operation I underwent when I was still in the hospital was for skin grafts on my legs. Skin from my abdomen was removed and put in a machine which meshed it into a window-screen-like patch which was then grafted onto the wounds on my legs. When I saw the results after the operation, I felt disappointed. Why couldn't my surgeon have covered more area? I thought.

True, my doctor had explained that new skin would grow back itself, but I must admit that I didn't believe him. I watched skeptically as the nurses scrubbed away the dead skin and removed it with tweezers. And within days we saw growing patches of new, white skin around the edges of the burn! Each day the gap in the middle got smaller and smaller until it was completely healed. How incredible it was! The doctor had been right.

❈   ❈   ❈

When all is well, people don't usually take the time to write to each other and express admiration, appreciation, and affection. Because of my circumstances, people were prompted to write and my heart was filled with gratitude at the many letters and gifts I received, many from people I had never met. Individuals from my hometown in Connecticut, as well as others in the U.S. and Israel who had read about me in newspaper accounts of the fire, generously wrote and expressed their feelings.

The fact that I saved my children seemed to be the catalyst, the focal point of a heroic story which inspired people. The suffering I was going through moved them to prayer and fasting and encouraged them to give charity. I felt this tremendous energy coming not only from my own community but from all over the world. Knowing that thousands of Jews from all segments of our Nation were acting for the benefit of my family and me was a wonderful feeling that I had never experienced before. Here are a few of the many letters I received.

Dear Malka,

You may be surprised to receive a letter from me....at first I could not write because it was just too soon...later it was enough to thank Hashem that you were making progress...and now I must write to tell you that my prayers have been added to the prayers of all those who care about Malka Shelly Smith-Abramson. We are legion!

For a while, it seemed that the Smith family et al were on the receiving end of more than it was possible for one family to bear. I hope that the knowledge of how many people do care is strengthening you. The things that have evolved from your ordeal are both frightening and inspiring at the same time....and I'm speaking as an outsider. It boggles the mind to think about how you must feel.

I can sort of imagine the pain. I can even imagine the fear. But I cannot imagine the mixture of it all plus the highs that must come over each small advancement. Your Mom keeps me informed of every one, whether I'm in Florida (as I am now) or at home.

And that's another thing. I can only marvel at the strength your folks have shown through this awesome trial. You picked yourself some set of parents!!

And your grandmother — she has been a brick through all this. Every time I saw her while she was still staying with your folks, she was learning new ways to cope, too.

Dearest Malka, we cannot know why terrible things happen. So often bitterness can be the bottom line of tragedy. But I feel somehow that your faith will not let that happen in your case. That's one of the things I pray for...

Love,

Sylvia

＊　＊　＊

My dearest Malka,

How can I begin to express to you what I felt when I heard of the tragedy that happened; and it is even more difficult to express the love and awe and pain that I felt for you when I heard of your super-human courage in saving your family... The vision of you carrying your children to safety remains alive for me, until this moment.

To speak of it as a tragedy does not seem real. I and many of our mutual friends here have relived that tragedy

(if one can in any way do that) as if it were our own, knowing (if in any way one can know) your pain. Malka, we pray
every day for your speedy recovery and for the moment
when you will be able to brighten our people's lives again
with your cheerful smile. I'm sure that you have heard by
now that I am engaged to be married (God willing) in less
than three weeks. I hope that news of this happy event will
also help to brighten your day, Malka. I hope that soon I
can bring my husband to meet you as we plan to return
to live in Eretz Yisrael. Malka, I wish you a speedy, speedy
recovery. I am honored to have you as a friend. Be strong
and know that all your friends are with you here.

With much love,

Hannah

❀   ❀   ❀

My dear Michele,

I was so sad to hear what happened to you. I know these
are tough times for you but I also know how much character you have and always had, and how brave you are.
I know you'll beat this thing. Somehow childhood friends
have a special place in my heart. You were always such a
special friend, Michele, with that captivating impish grin and
that sense of love and life. You always had a certain glow...
Remember, Michele, that a lot of your old friends in
America are praying for your quick recovery. You have
that unique quality that seems to touch people. They don't
forget you. We all love you and I am sure before you know
it you'll be back on your feet. Lots of love to your family,
sister and parents. If I can do anything to help let me know.

Love,

Lenny

❀   ❀   ❀

My parents were with me and at Nana's side throughout the most difficult weeks. Their kindness and devotion
knew no bounds. Indeed, all their lives they had been
involved in acts of kindness in the Jewish community. My
mother had always been active in Hadassah projects and
my father in fundraising events for the Hebrew Free Loan
Association.

Their kindness extended to the smallest details of
personal attention as well. Once I asked them if they
could bring me one hundred white envelopes to fit the
Rosh Hashanah cards that I had designed and had printed
here in Israel. When they arrived on their annual visit to
us, they brought the envelopes along with all the other
thoughtful gifts, and I thanked them happily. It was only
later that I learned the extent of their dedication. It seems
that they had not been able to find the size of envelopes
that I had asked for, so they bought a larger size, and then,
with Nana, stayed up half the night cutting and pasting
them by hand, to make them the size I had requested.
I was astounded that it had meant so much to them to
fulfill my request.

One day in the hospital when I was taken out of my
room in a wheelchair, I glanced up at the glass partition
and I was stunned at my reflection. Every day my parents
saw their child completely bandaged from head to toe!
They had never shown the slightest sign of how hard it
surely must have been for them to see me like this — not
to mention seeing my grandmother's suffering as well.

❄ ❄ ❄

Later, after the critical weeks were past, I wondered
why no one had come to hold my hand and prepare me
for death, to say the *Vidui,* the final confession. I used
to think that a person who has a short time to live should
be told, so that he can prepare himself properly. In retro-
spect, I see it differently. Our Sages said that a person

should not give up hope even if the sword is at his throat, because Hashem's salvation can come in the winking of an eye. We've all heard miraculous stories of how people have been saved from the jaws of death at the very last minute.

From what I have observed, a spiritual person senses when his end is going to be and no one has to tell him. After I had survived those first three days, I believed I would live. I wasn't really aware of all the whirlwind around me, all the concern for my life, and I believe that was the best thing. Not knowing the morbid statistics, that I'd been given one chance in ten of surviving, I remained hopeful and inspired. Positive thinking is a crucial element of healing and recovery. I simply believed that Hashem would answer my prayers for life. It is said that when a person decides to go in a particular direction, an angel is created to help him.

One of the first things the Rabbi did, along with calling for the recital of *Tehillim*, was to gather a *minyan* to change my name. There is a tradition among some to change the name of a dangerously ill person, so that we can in effect say to Hashem that if death has been decreed for so-and-so, that so-and-so is not the same person; he has another name, and the decree doesn't apply. Often a name from the Hebrew root connoting "life" is added to one's name. As a child, *Michele* became *Shelly*. In later years I liked using *Michele* again. Now, five years after changing *Michele* to my Hebrew name, *Malka*, I had another name. What would my parents think? They had finally gotten used to calling me Malka — and now I was Chaya Malka. Once my name was changed, I felt a strong responsibility to use both names. In recognition of the decision of the Rabbi who added the name of "Life," I made sure to call myself Chaya Malka.

In those early, difficult weeks, when I was suffering greatly, a friend, Rachel, came to the hospital to spend each Shabbat with me. We sang Shabbat songs together, she made *Kiddush*, and she read to me from the weekly Torah portion. In the warmth of her kind and friendly smile, I found peace of mind. She was humble and didn't demand much. It was not like having visitors, when I had to muster energy that I didn't always have. She was soothing and undemanding. The nurses were generally too busy to sit down and chat with me, but I didn't need it, for speaking with Rachel was enough, and always inspiring. Like the extra soul we receive on Shabbat, Hashem sent me the gift of Rachel's company.

Professor Menachem Ron Wexler, my plastic surgeon, is a man with special warmth and refinement of character. His words are greatly valued and what he says is always said so pleasantly. After the first six weeks were over he said to Simcha, "We've done everything for Chaya Malka that medicine can do." Then he paused. "Let me tell you what my teacher once asked me when I was a small child: 'Tell me, Menachem Ron, have you said the special blessing today that we say every morning, thanking our Creator for making our bodies work properly?'" (Blessed are You... Who fashioned man with wisdom and created within him many openings and many cavities...)

Hashem used His wisdom to create man: the exact balance of our organs and their functions demonstrates this. Amazingly, our spiritual soul fuses with the physical body to form the whole person. Professor Wexler, in his gentle, inimitable manner, was telling Simcha that he should pray with intent and purpose, for as he saw it now, my recovery was in the hands of Hashem. It is written in the Gemara that a person cannot risk his life and rely on a miracle to save him, but if one is in danger and there is no way out, one must pray for a miracle, go beyond what is humanly possible, to the supra-natural, *l'malah min ha-teva*. It was a great comfort knowing that Professor Wexler was the kind of doctor who recognized our reliance on Hashem.

My Nana was discharged from the hospital after six weeks, at the same point at which I was taken off the critical list. My miraculous and quick recovery was due in part to the fact that I had suffered no damage to my lungs or other internal organs. My parents felt relieved and confident that they were leaving me in good hands and could take Nana home with them. She had made many friends at the Yeshiva during her annual visits to Miriam and me, and our friends had made sure to visit her in the hospital too. Now Nana was ready to go back to the States where my parents could take care of her in the comfort of their own home. Nana suffered thirty-five percent burns and was in a lot of pain. She remained under a doctor's care for many months in my parents' home. It was not until three years had passed that she was able to come back with my mother for a joyful reunion with her granddaughters and great-grandchildren.

It was on a Shabbat that I sat up by myself for the first time. I was alone in my hospital room when it happened. The joy of sitting up by myself was indescribable, and my independence seemed nothing less than a miracle. I did it without help in the most natural and effortless way. It was a step forward and a blessing comparable only to the first time I moved the first joint of my index finger and the first time I moved my thumb. It was the result of all the work that had gone on before. Each day a veritable army of physiotherapists and occupational therapists would come to work on me — moving my hands, my fingers, and my legs for me. I was unable to do anything on my own, even feed myself. It wasn't that I was paralyzed; it was just that the pain of moving and the extreme lack of muscle tone combined to make it impossible to move easily by myself. Normal skin has a quality of elasticity which grafted skin lacks; healing grafted skin needs constant motion to keep it supple enough that it will not contract.

Each morning upon awakening, the first prayer we recite is *Modeh ani lefanecha...* — "I gratefully thank you, O living and eternal King, for You have returned my soul within me with compassion — abundant is your faithfulness!" When I opened my eyes in the hospital every morning, it was with special poignance that I thanked Hashem for restoring my faculties to me and acknowledged that He did so in expectation that I would serve Him and that He is abundantly faithful to reward those who do. When something is taken away and then returned, one feels more appreciative of the found object. I was overwhelmed with the feeling of gratefulness.

When I walked by myself for the first time, I was encouraged and helped by the nurses. My legs felt so heavy, tingling, and uncomfortable, that I couldn't imagine how they'd hold me. Supporting myself on the mobile I.V. stand, I was afraid I would fall — even though I never did.

The dependence on others during the process of my recovery made me feel like a big baby. I needed a lot of encouragement to recover my faculties, to be able to function again as a wife and mother. An infant is born helpless, dependent in every way on his mother and his family. I too was totally dependent on Hashem and on those around me, the nurses, the doctors, and my family who came to the hospital to help me. Though in a sense I felt reborn by having to go through these stages of development again, I understood there was a difference. An infant instinctively goes through the stages of development, slowly becoming more independent each day, each month, each year. He cannot express in words, nor does he have the need to, what it feels like to sit up for the very first time or even walk by himself.

To experience these stages of development again as a fully aware adult is to appreciate what a gift it is just to be normal. Each time I had more skin grafted onto my legs, they had to be put into casts for three days. The half-casts enhanced the success of the operation by keeping my legs absolutely still and stationary. While not moving for three days was great for the healing of my skin graft, however, it was terrible for my muscles and blood circulation. Three times I had to undergo the procedure of the skin-graft operation on my legs followed by three days of immobility. Each time I'd think, Do I really have to go through this again? Just when I'm seeing the results of all my efforts? All right, I accept it — I'll sit up — I'll try to stand with two nurses helping me up... I'll manage the pain. It wasn't as if I had to learn to walk all over again, because my brain already knew the pattern of walking from experience. Teaching the muscles and tendons to move again was very painful, and I felt like a rusty old bicycle that needed oiling. I would have to work hard to recover my strength and coordination.

One of the nurses was especially insistent about getting me to do things by myself and she tried to teach me to feed myself — a really amazing thing — when it seemed to me almost impossible. The occupational therapist tried to figure out what kind of utensil would be appropriate for my needs, and then adjust it. For example, they would fit a cylinder of sponge around the stem of my fork or spoon so I could grasp and control it. At the beginning, every bite was a struggle, and it was extremely frustrating.

When Miriam would come and want to feed me, the nurse would object adamantly. "No! Your sister is now feeding herself." Sometimes the food spilled before it reached my mouth, and I fought back tears of frustration. "Hashem," I prayed silently, "help me. Please don't let me be ashamed." Ultimately I told myself there was only one thing to do: try even harder. Once when my father was visiting, he watched as I put food on the spoon and then tried to get it into my mouth. It took ages, and Dad suddenly realized that the spoon was too large to fit into my bandaged mouth. He hurried to town and brought back a few spoons that were smaller and able to fit into my mouth better.

When I became exhausted after struggling to feed myself for about fifteen minutes, I was allowed to be fed by my sister or my Dad who were waiting close by to help. At this time I was emaciated due to rapid loss of calories, for part of the function of the skin is to retain body heat and where there is no skin to retain heat, calories get burned up rapidly. While I was healing I didn't gain any weight and I had no appetite. To guarantee that I was getting the proper nutrition and to fatten me up a bit, I was given a high-calorie protein drink called *Ensure* a few times a day. At first I looked forward to what seemed to be a milkshake treat, and I actually enjoyed it. As time passed, however, it became more and more a chalky medicine that was difficult to swallow.

From the very first day, Miriam was at my side. At the beginning, when no one knew whether I would live, I can only imagine how my sister, my one and only sibling, must have felt. Hashem sends us special people to help us during difficult times in our lives and my sister was one such Heaven-sent person. My brother-in-law Ben Zion was selfless in his support of her and her daily treks to the hospital to help me in every possible way. She put all her time and energy into making me comfortable in the hope that her efforts might contribute to my survival. Of course only the Almighty can ultimately save anyone, but she tried to do what she could.

Because she was a nurse, Miriam thought she would be able to help me a lot but the hospital staff wouldn't really let her do anything. They had their own techniques. She had heard about the wonders of honey in healing skin, for example, but even though we were both believers in natural medicine, we decided to leave it up to the doctors. "Our best bet is to rely on modern medicine, together with our prayers and the tremendous emotional support of the community," she said. I agreed.

While the community was involved in getting my family settled at home, Miriam was totally involved in taking care of me at the hospital. Before I could swallow solid food, and to supplement the chemical formula the hospital provided, she would make me fresh almond milkshakes and vegetable juices. I know that sometimes she was disappointed to find the milkshakes hardly touched on my bedside table when she arrived in the morning. She prepared them lovingly and brought them to the hospital fresh each day so every vitamin would be retained. I could not bring myself to tell her that on some days I had no appetite at all, but she could see for herself.

I think that the greatest thing I learned from my whole experience was the ability to appreciate. On one of Miriam's regular visits to me I confided, "You know, the doctors say they cannot believe that I am here in this world...they can't believe how well I'm doing."

"You just have Hashem on your side, Malka," she answered. "A person who has the will to live comes through."

❋ ❋ ❋

King David said, "This nation (Israel) is distinguished by three characteristics: They are merciful, bashful, and kind" (*Yevamos* 79a). I learned from our Rabbi that there are two categories of *chesed*, as defined in the Torah. One kind knocks at your door — whether it is a person asking for charity, a loan, or a cup of sugar, one should stop what he is doing and turn his attention to fulfilling another's needs. (Our Rabbi used to say that if people are not knocking at your door, you have to think seriously about the reason.) The second form of *chesed* has to be run after and grabbed. If you don't grab it, it runs away from you.

I was fortunate enough to recognize this second kind of *chesed* in my dear friend Leah. She always made herself available to anyone who needed her help. This was an admirable quality and I wanted to emulate it. When the phone call came, telling her of my accident, she moved into high gear and took upon herself the responsibility of organizing all the different tasks that the situation demanded. For the six long weeks that I remained in critical condition, there was tremendous tension in our community, but everyday life had to go on. All the work that a woman does in her home had to be done by others for my family: cooking, grocery shopping, washing and ironing clothes, caring for the needs of the children, buying school supplies and clothing, to name a few. Leah took care to iron out the creases in the cloth of life, and she made sure my home was running smoothly.

One day after my midmorning nap, I awoke to find Leah sitting quietly at my bedside, holding a *siddur* and engrossed in prayer. Her eyes met mine and I felt the deep warmth that had bonded us when we were neighbors on Mount Zion. I had so many questions to ask her now! I wanted to know how it was decided that Esther would stay in the Jewish Quarter. I wanted to know her thoughts on the fire, and its effects on the community.

Leah herself was hesitant to bring up these painful subjects but she agreed to tell me after I convinced her that I needed to know for my own peace of mind.

"It was six in the morning and dark," she began, as she placed her *Tehillim* book on the table. "When the phone began ringing so early, I guess I dreaded hearing bad news. It was Sima, who sounded very upset. She said you had burned your hands and that I should go to the hospital. It didn't sound so bad to me, almost as if the fire was worse than the burns. Since Simcha was away, though, I figured you'd want me to babysit for the kids. I just didn't realize that you were badly burned — until I got to the hospital.

"When the situation became known, there were a lot of practical things to take care of. First of all, there were so many calls coming in to the Yeshiva — offers of help — that I thought the best thing to do was to channel our energies into practical arrangements. Right away the issue was who was going to take care of your kids. They had gone off to nursery school that morning after being checked at the clinic. It wasn't as if decisions were made in a logical way. It was more like a chain reaction, one action effecting the next.

"When Simcha came back we heard that he and the kids were going to move into the downstairs complex of Yeshiva apartments. When he realized that he wouldn't be able to take care of Esther like a mother would, your friend Sarah just stepped forward and volunteered to take care of the baby. She and her husband saw a personal need and wanted to help. The next day a few neighbors brought Esther's crib over to their apartment in the Jewish Quarter."

Leah paused for a moment. "You know, I discussed it with our pediatrician. I asked him about the possible problems inherent in other people taking care of a baby in Esther's situation for an extended period of time, and he assured me that it was an excellent solution. He said, for example, that in a big family in which a grandmother, older sisters, and aunts all take care of a baby, in addition to the mother, the baby will go to all of them when he needs something. To the baby all these older women are 'mother figures.' Even when he learns that each one of them has a name, they remain mother figures. The baby does not love his mother less because he loves the others and turns to them too. His conclusion was that Esther would benefit most of all by having a nurturing mother figure in a family setting even if it is not her own, that this would give her the security she needs now.

"And I can assure you, Esther is doing just fine," Leah said. "She'll be in good hands until you come home to take care of her yourself."

"Thank you, Leah," I said quietly, feeling my burden of anxiety about my baby lift. I took a deep breath. "I really needed to hear that. Now tell me, what about the apartment? I really want to know."

"There were priorities," she continued. "After arrangements for meals and children and finding a place to live were taken care of, we went into the burnt apartment to see what the situation was. It really looked terrible, as you can imagine, but when we went through it, we realized that a lot more was salvageable than we'd thought. A lot of things were just water-damaged, not fire-damaged: they needed to be laundered, or sent to the dry cleaners, or in the case of toys, to be washed. We thought it was important that the kids have as many familiar things around them as possible — their own clothes, their own toys, and their own beds."

I nodded, speechless. My friends were no less concerned about my family than I was.

"Then we fixed whatever furniture we could. Oh, and Chaya Malka, you know what? Someone took the job of putting your photo albums back in shape. Clothing is something that can always be replaced, but personal items like photographs, recipe files, and letters can't, so instinctively people tried their best to save things like that. It was really all spontaneous — people would call and offer help, all the time. There were meals prepared every day. It seemed more practical to have the same person make the same type of meal on the same day of the week: Mondays, spaghetti; Tuesdays, fish, etc. For the kids, we felt that routine and consistency were the most important things of all.

"Your in-laws and parents, Chaya Malka, were there from the first day, providing constant loving family care for the kids every afternoon after nursery school. They are really amazing. They also brought kitchen supplies for the new apartment and everything that's needed for daily living. So you see, your kids have their schedule, they have their spaghetti, they take their baths, every day is routinely the same."

The sheer amount of *chesed* we were receiving overwhelmed me. Leah went on matter-of-factly, "You know, Barbara, the social worker, had told us in the emergency room on the morning of the fire, 'I'm here for you. Call on me if you need me.' Well, the next morning was very foggy, and the fog looked like smoke at first to the kids. They were very frightened when they saw it. I thought to myself, These kids have been through a lot and I'm not sure how to help them. Your sister Miriam, our close circle of neighbors, and I were all feeling the stress of the situation.

"I decided to call Barbara at home that night. 'Listen,' I said, 'I don't know how to handle the situation well. The kids are frightened and I think we need your professional help.' Barbara was amazing — she came right over, up to Mount Zion, sat down and helped us. She met with the kids, encouraged them to talk, and reassured them."

"I really appreciate that," I said. "You've all done great *chesed* for us, Leah."

"I think *chesed* is just a part of the Jewish personality," Leah replied. "It's part of the Jewish soul." Leah suddenly sensed how exhausted I had become. She leaned over and kissed me goodbye.

❄   ❄   ❄

One morning I noticed a certain excitement among the nurses in the Burn Unit. They were bustling about polishing, cleaning, and rearranging the furniture in my room. As they straightened my blankets and fluffed my pillows, I asked one of them what all the excitement was about.

"Oh, Chaya Malka, Hadassah Hospital is about to have a very honored guest — the wife of the President of Israel, Mrs. Ophira Navon," she said breathlessly. "In fact, she's expected to arrive in our ward any minute!"

Suddenly my door opened and there she was, beautiful and elegant, holding a huge arrangement of flowers that she had brought just for me. Mrs. Navon didn't seem at all flustered about seeing me wrapped like a mummy. Smiling, she accepted me as I was and that comforted me. I was presented with the extravagant bouquet as a heroine who had been willing to sacrifice her life on the battlefield — even though I didn't relate to myself that way.

I felt her genuine compassion when she said, "Your rescue of your family and your stoic acceptance of your pain are shining examples for all of us." I was overwhelmed, especially since I knew that certain acquaintances of mine, afraid of what they might see, couldn't yet bring themselves to come and visit. They were afraid to face a friend who might not make it. They were afraid of doing more damage than good by their emotional state. It was therefore all the more overwhelming to see Mrs. Navon, may she rest in peace, come and visit and appear entirely nonplused by my appearance.

Another celebrity who often came to see me was Simcha Holtzberg, who was known as "the Father of the Wounded." He was a living legend who visited, brought gifts, arranged simchas and celebrations, and comforted wounded soldiers and civilian victims of terrorist attacks, in hospitals all over Israel. It was known that he would often accompany burned patients into the chamber of the dreaded bath. There, as they cried out in pain during their treatments, he would comfort them as a father would his own son. He was always on hand to reassure worried relatives, and he remained in touch with casualties throughout their recovery.

He always arrived with a cheerful expression, followed by an entourage of young soldiers singing and dancing, handing out candy, nuts, and chocolates. He was said to live with daily memories of the Holocaust, and he would tell people that all disabled veterans were now his extended family — he had lost his own to the Nazis. Even though I was obviously not a soldier, Mr. Holtzberg, of blessed memory, considered me a heroine and treated me like one.

Fortunate is one when the God of Yaakov is his help, whose hope is in Hashem his God.

TEHILLIM 146:5

THREE MONTHS AFTER the fire, there was talk among the nurses of moving me to the "going home room." This room would be used to prepare me for my eventual discharge from the hospital. Professor Wexler had originally told me my hospital stay would probably be for a period of at least six months — and here I was after only three months being transferred to a room from where I would be sent home.

My new room had fewer machines, a private bathroom, and was in general much more homey. I eventually spent what felt like a very long month there before I was finally sent home for a brief Purim holiday.

One evening in the hospital I heard that my talented women friends would be giving a concert at the end of the hall. As chairs were set up in a semicircle, I hobbled over to a place they had prepared for me. The musicians took their places and the sounds of guitars and drums began to fill the ward as interested staff members and patients were drawn to this curious sight. How enjoyable it was! Their sweet melodies lifted my spirits, took me out of the hospital routine, and helped me forget my pains, if only for a short while. In my heart I thanked Hashem for this special evening with such caring friends.

It was at this time that I began to wear a Jobst pressure suit, in order to prevent my scars from becoming elevated and disfigured. The suit, manufactured in the United States, had been recently introduced in Jerusalem as a viable form of burn treatment after successful use in Haifa. I was measured in the hospital by a representative of the Jobst Company for a perfect fit, to the exact millimeter.

The outfit consisted of an elastic pressure suit which encased the entire body, a head and face mask with openings for the eyes, nostrils, mouth, and ears; a jacket closing at the back with Velcro; tights from waist to ankle; and a pair of gloves. Each suit cost hundreds of dollars. Since I had to order a new suit each time my body changed — when swelling had gone down, or I had gained or lost weight — I was fitted numerous times. In addition, a wonderful woman who worked in the occupational therapy room patiently altered each new suit according to my exact present size. Since it took a month to fill the order, my measurements had often changed again. The gloves were always the hardest to fit.

Putting the suit on felt as if I were getting dressed for a deep-sea dive. But there was more to it than just struggling to get it on. Wherever the suit did not assert enough pressure on my scars, pieces of sponge had to be put in for that purpose: they were inserted behind my knees, inside my elbows, and under my chin. Getting dressed and undressed to take a daily shower was a test of patience, an ordeal I would have to go through for the next two years.

Someone had to dress me in the skin-tight suit for at least a year and a half because my hands were not strong enough to do the job alone. It was a tedious project, literally inching on the suit. In the beginning, the nurses and therapists did not know how to put it on me, how to get the skin-tight, tiny garment onto my body with the least amount of pain. The first time they put it on inside out and backwards! Then we figured out how to do it the right way, slowly inching it up each arm and then pulling it over my head. It had to be literally stretched on. It was a real team effort.

During the healing period, I suffered terrible itching. There was special Vitamin E cream available to alleviate it, but unfortunately the Vitamin E oil in the cream could destroy the elastic in the suit. Therefore I had a choice: to either wear the suit without the cream and suffer torturous itching of the new skin regenerating under the suit or not to wear the suit and remain disfigured by terrible scars but alleviate the itching of my healing skin. I was told that burn victims like myself sometimes commit suicide, or go crazy, or become recluses because of their terrible disfigurement. None of the possibilities was an option for me, so I went on wearing my artificial skin — and itching. At one point when I couldn't stand the itching any longer, I took the suit off for two weeks. I developed so many scars and swirls during that period, however, that I decided I would just have to put up with the itching. It was really shocking: not only were the new scars ugly and hard but some had already become raised swirls of skin which shortened my range of movement. "That's it!" I told myself. "The Jobst suit must be put back on." Now it would have an additional function, to flatten the scars down to the first skin level. It became clear then what a wonderful job the suit was doing and somehow I was able to bear the itching again for the next year and a half. I was the first severely burned woman to wear the suit and the treatment proved very successful. Although the scars that had formed never disappeared completely, the suit smoothed them out.

❋ ❋ ❋

Simcha was scheduled to play in the Chasidic Song

Festival, which would be held in the Binyanei Ha-Umah convention hall. I was disappointed that I wouldn't be able to attend.

"Why not go?" my friends asked during a visit to me in the hospital.

"But how would I manage?" I replied. "What would I wear?" Since most of my clothes had been destroyed in the fire, they reassured me that they would shop for something that would fit all my new requirements. I was excited at the prospect. "First of all," I told them, "since my skin is super-sensitive, the dress will have to be a non-irritating fabric like cotton. The sleeves have to be loose enough to fit these large clumsy splints I'm wearing. I'll need a zipper or possibly Velcro closings so I can put it on myself." How fortunate I felt to have friends like these who went to the trouble of shopping for me so I could have the pleasure of attending Simcha's concert.

After working in fashion design for many years, I'd always enjoyed putting clothes together in a creative way. Now, even though I had to wear the mask and the pressure suit all the time, somehow I imagined wearing a special outfit. Thus it was very humbling for me to go out in the simple house dress, which fit all the requirements, that my devoted friends purchased for me.

The night of the concert finally arrived. I had never imagined I could just pick up and leave the hospital for an evening out. But with my friends' help, we were soon in our family car riding along with Simcha in the cool Jerusalem night. Since my husband had performed for many years in annual Chasidic Song Festivals, it felt familiar being backstage with him and the rest of the band before the show. And once the concert began, the lights dimmed, and on stage the musicians began the performance, I knew my husband was playing his clarinet just for me. During the intermission, I remember walking up the aisle in my mask, suit, and hand splints feeling as if I had been let out of jail for the first time. One moment it was doctors, nurses, white walls, and hospital equipment, and the next, a happy vibrating crowd full of life, songs and action. I did not feel awkward or self-conscious because people seemed so preoccupied with the concert and with socializing that they hardly noticed me. It was as if I were in an invisible bubble, something like what I had read in Rashi's commentary in the Book of Yehoshua, about Pinchas' visit to Rachav.

❊ ❊ ❊

Menucha, a friend of the family, came to visit, bringing me a beautiful scarf that her mother had knitted. I was grateful and surprised, and thanked her. But I was speechless when she asked me to give her a blessing. Silence filled the room as I tried to absorb the meaning of her request. A blessing from *me*? I was only a simple, ordinary person. Why, people would set out early in the morning to travel to the city of Netivot in southern Israel, and stand in line for hours in the Negev heat to receive a blessing from the great *tzaddik* who lived there. And what about the blessing of the *Kohanim* on Shabbat that we all receive when we stand in the synagogue?

Where did I fit in? I knew that people saw me as a heroine but I didn't understand how a heroine was supposed to give a blessing! I confessed I didn't know what to say — so, puppet-like, embarrassed and confused, I gave her the blessings she asked for.

❊ ❊ ❊

Clara, the head nurse who had been instrumental in making my first visit with my children a success, told me that I was going to be discharged from the hospital for three days — in time for the Purim holiday. I was anxious, frightened, and at the same time thrilled at the thought of going home. I couldn't imagine how I would manage, and

I became extremely worried about the threat of infection which was still hanging over my head.

Running from storage cabinet to medicine shelves, she excitedly brought me an assortment of special sterile bandages, salves, and pills that I would need during my three days at home. And then, sitting at my bedside, she explained patiently, gently, and in great detail, how I was to use everything that she had collected for me. Clara reassured me that I would be just fine and that nothing bad would happen to me once I left the hospital. She was not only knowledgeable and efficient in her work, but she was also warm and kind in her manner, knowing how to be authoritative with a smile on her face. Such self-confidence left me no room to argue that maybe I was not yet ready to leave the hospital. I trusted her. I was reminded of King Solomon's words: "The words of the wise spoken gently are heard..." (*Kohelet* 9:17). Because Clara's logic was sound and her character strong she did not need firm words to reassure me.

The day finally came when my husband drove me home for my first three days away from the Burn Unit. I was wearing a long green velour robe over my Jobst suit and a matching green scarf over my head mask. The scarf and robe which matched perfectly, were both gifts from close friends. It was great to be wearing them, but inside the mask, I felt uncomfortable and confined, as if my head were being pressed between the two ends of a clamp. And although I enjoyed the new green scarf, I thought that my head was surely sufficiently covered with three hundred and sixty degrees of pressure. My friends wanted me to "appear more normal," so for them I wore the scarf — even though inside I felt a little silly.

Looking out the car window, I was affected deeply by the great variety of things we passed on our way home. I hadn't seen a tree in months; in the hospital, most things that surrounded me had smooth bland lines; and even the big window in the "going home" room looked out onto a large paved courtyard and an endless sky. It was exciting now to observe all the different scenes as we drove through the winding country roads of Ein Kerem. Every street was different, and every house had its own distinctive garden.

"Could anyone imagine that a garbage can could be such a wonderful sight?" I blurted out to Simcha from my own world in the back seat of our car. Trees bent in the wind, there were changes of light in the cloudy sky, and the wind blew against my face mask as we sped along. Just as I had been apprehensive about how I would be able to manage for three days at home, away from the security of the hospital, I imagined Simcha was preoccupied now with his own thoughts of what it would be like taking responsibility for my care.

My excitement mounted as we slowly ascended the road to Mount Zion. The car suddenly stopped at the front gate of our new apartment. "Last stop," my husband said cheerfully. "Everybody out!" I felt like an old lady trying to get out of the car. My every move was strained and uncomfortable. I slowly ascended the seven steps, and, as I reached the top, I whispered to myself, "This is going to take longer than I thought." I began the slow walk along the path to my door. I was coming home to a house I didn't know. The small studio apartment was on the ground floor in the middle of a complex of eight other homes occupied by my friends and their families at the Yeshiva. They would become my support system for the next few years.

Of all the gifts that I received, one of my favorites was a framed drawing of our new neighborhood on Mount Zion with all the neighbors and their children standing with their doors open wide, welcoming me home. Everyone had signed the picture with personal well-wishing comments. Now, as I approached the apartment, I looked around, and the scene which greeted me was very different from the beautiful drawing of my homecoming that my friend had made for me. In the dreamlike picture each doorway was filled with laughing children and their parents waving to me. It seemed unusually quiet in our neighborhood. I looked at the clear blue sky and heard the sound of birds chirping in the trees. The neighborhood children were in school and nursery school. It felt deserted compared to the hustle and bustle of the hospital. I imagined that maybe, of all those faces that were in the drawing, some were peeking out at me from behind their windows now. Together with a little disappointment, it was also a relief to arrive home unnoticed, as it took tremendous emotional energy for me just to walk up the path with splints on my arms and a mask on my face. My close friends were probably staying away so that I could experience these private moments alone with my husband. And they were right; it was enough to have myself to deal with in my new surroundings.

I took a deep breath as I prepared to enter the home I didn't know. Slowly I walked in, looking around. Everything in the tiny apartment was new to me! And how clean and neat the house appeared. But I didn't feel like a visitor at all — this was where I belonged. People from all over the country had donated furniture and housewares, from the beds to the tablecloth, yet I felt a total acceptance of it all. My children's artwork decorated the walls, their pictures providing a pleasant warm and homey feeling. My neighbors had played an integral part in giving the house such a wonderful appearance.

Erev Purim was always an exciting time. Our neighbors invited us, as in previous years, to join them for the festive Purim *seudah.* In the past, we had always shared the responsibility of preparing the meal, but this year

My first visit home, for Purim: Esther in her Purim costume and me in my Jobst suit.

I was thrilled just to be sharing their company. Purim morning brought the usual flurry of activity, with the morning's reading of the Scroll of Esther, and the sending of *mishlo'ach manot* to neighbors. It reminded me of the packages of sweets, fruits, and wine that we had prepared last year, and of all the things I used to do with my family for the holiday. Besides preparing the festive meal and sending gifts, I'd always loved creating Purim costumes for my children to wear — and also for myself and Simcha. *B'ezrat Hashem*, I told myself, next year... This year just experiencing Purim was overwhelming.

In our neighborhood we have a second reading of the *Megillah* on Purim night, for those women who didn't hear the first reading in the *beit knesset* earlier. I attended the second reading, and I was surprised when I was chosen for the honor of reciting the blessing of *She-hecheyanu* aloud, one of the three blessings recited before the reading begins.

As I stood up, surrounded by my closest friends, and

said this special blessing, I was overwhelmed. I had never said it before with such joy. It should only be so that we should feel this thankful every day of our lives, I thought. Tears filled my eyes as I said the words of this blessing of life, praising Hashem, "Who has kept us alive and sustained us."

✻   ✻   ✻

The Purim activities going on all around me seemed to be moving at a very fast pace, too fast. I was inundated with new experiences — not at all like my daily hospital routine. For one thing, I wasn't used to sitting in one place for a long time. I had to keep my elbow and knee joints constantly moving to keep my healing skin from tightening into a contracted position.

When I was in the hospital a young woman named Galit had come to visit me. When she entered my room her reddish-brown hair, which framed her pretty face, caught my eye. Galit had suffered burns in a terrible accident while serving in the army. She rolled up her shirt sleeves and showed me deep and severe scars on her arms. As a result of her neglecting to exercise enough, according to her doctors' instructions, her right arm had contracted into a ninety degree immobile angle. She was scheduled to undergo surgery in an attempt to enable her arm to be mobile again. The Jobst gloves she wore on her hands had no benefit after all this time had passed; she wore them, she explained, only to hide her scars which she couldn't bear to see. It was very sad to hear, and to see, how she was having such difficulties. Her visits had a tremendous impact on me and from then on I was extremely careful to do everything the doctors had instructed.

I knew that accepting oneself is crucial in order to go forward. I became one hundred percent dedicated to helping myself. From that moment on, as long as I was awake I never stopped exercising. When I was walking, I made sure that my hands were moving, and when I was sitting, my legs were swinging under my chair.

As I sat at our Purim *seudah*, I was a very strange sight. The guests were sitting around the table enjoying their festive meal, and there I was in my mask and body suit, looking like a toy bear, drumming my fingers and swinging my legs. It looked bizarre but I didn't care. I was determined to keep doing everything to enhance the healing process.

At the beautifully set Purim table, I found myself partaking of a delicious meal. Even though sitting up was physically trying, it was a tremendous relief to be there. There was the joy of the family, the smiling faces of friends, and everyone singing and laughing together.

Although I still had no appetite during that first visit home, I was always happy to sit at the table for three meals a day with my family. The mask that I always wore was expressionless, a little scary, and like being behind a steel door. Since I had to remove it to eat, this was an excellent opportunity to communicate with all the appropriate facial expressions. How I hated having to put the mask back on!

The word was out that I was home for Purim. The day afterwards a lot of people came to visit me. I enjoyed the first few visitors but as the afternoon wore on and the streams of visitors continued to appear, I began to suffer, to feel like a monkey in the zoo that everyone had come to stare at. I knew I had a peculiar appearance, but my discomfort welled up in me until at one point I burst out, "Please, no more visitors! Enough! Go away, everybody!"

What had happened? I'd never imagined it would be that way. But then again, I never anticipated how painful it would be when people stared. I was shocked. Why couldn't they control their behavior? I thought. And they seemed frightened at what they saw. I didn't expect *that* from adults. In the hospital, I was the hostess and they were my guests. There I was prepared, and I tried to reassure them. But here at home, I just couldn't bear the pain and embarrassment of their stares.

The first night home was also difficult, and there were many little things that I had not anticipated. First of all, there was no buzzer to call the night nurse! In fact, there was no night nurse. I felt bad waking up my husband in the middle of the night to help me to the bathroom. But I was helpless. I would have liked to fly to the bathroom rather than hobble along with his help. I was weighted down by the half-leg casts which I had to wear at night. Another time I had to wake him up and ask him to smooth out a crease on my sheet which my very sensitive skin couldn't bear. Simcha didn't mind at all — he was always happy to help me. But although he never complained, somehow I was always apologizing anyway. I had to accept the fact that I would be needing people's help for some time.

❄ ❄ ❄

When I was still in the hospital, my neighbor Chava told me how much she was waiting for me to come home. And when I came home, she made it very easy for me to ask for her help if I needed it. Nothing was ever a burden for her. Whenever I would make apologies for having disturbed her sleep or taken her away from her family, she brushed it off as no problem at all. She insisted that I continue to call her for anything, at any hour of the day or night — which literally meant calling out the window, since our adjoining houses shared the same tiny courtyard. I learned from Chava how important it is to help others, with an attitude of genuine happiness and willingness.

❄ ❄ ❄

During the entire four months I spent in the hospital, I suffered from chronic high fever, for which the doctors never found the cause. As soon as I left the hospital, the bouts of fever stopped and never returned. The reason remained a mystery. When I was first allowed to leave the hospital, I was worried about catching a cold, getting a sore throat, or just getting sick in general, since it was winter time. Amazingly, though, during the next two years of my recovery I never once suffered from any of the common ailments young mothers are exposed to. Looking back, I felt Hashem was protecting my health because He knew just how much I could handle, and no more. I was dealing daily with great emotional and physical adjustments and this period of grace was another one of the Almighty's great gifts of *chesed.*

※　※　※

Being the center of constant attention for so long, I had become self-centered. Engrossed in the role of a sick, dependent person, I became demanding and assertive whenever I wanted something. Not only had my body changed, my personality seemed to have changed as well. Hashem provides certain safety factors which protect and help us in emergency situations, but my situation was no longer a critical one. When I finally came home, I continued to ask for assistance in a manner that suggested my needs were always an emergency and had to be dealt with immediately. It took a caring and tactful friend to gently point out to me that things weren't critical anymore, that I was home and could relax a bit. Now I had to readjust from dealing with doctors and nurses and new, unfamiliar faces to dealing with friends and family, forming and renewing long-lasting relationships.

When my brief Purim vacation was over, I remember that I felt a bit relieved going back to the Burn Unit. True, the taste of home was great, but I still had intensive physical and occupational therapy sessions to complete. And I felt secure being taken care of. But, like a fledgling gently pushed out of the nest, three weeks after my Purim visit at home, I found myself fully discharged from the hospital and home again. This time too, I experienced a kaleidoscope of feelings. As I neared my house, some children who were playing nearby saw me approaching and ran away in fright. I was grateful that my own children had become adjusted to my strange appearance during their regular visits to the hospital over the past four months. Once I put my face mask on in front of them so they would not be afraid. Devorah, Shua, and little Esther had watched in fascination as their mother transformed herself into a mannequin-like figure. Even though I looked bizarre to others, my children continued to accept me as before.

A good Jewish housewife usually begins her Pesach preparations at least a month before the actual holiday arrives. In the hospital, I was too preoccupied with getting through each day's treatments to even think about such things. Little did I know that a wonderful woman named Judith and her staff of volunteer workers at the hospital were concerned about how our family was going to manage for Passover once I got home. With the help of Simcha Holtzberg and others, she had been busy traveling around Israel to various factories collecting donations of all kinds — new pots, housewares, and holiday clothing — since our household possessions had been destroyed by the fire. After I had been home for a day or two, Judith called and said she would like to come and visit. As I always enjoyed her company, I looked forward to seeing her again. A few hours later there was a knock at the door, and there was Judith, all smiles and eager to show me the contents of her red car parked outside, which was overflowing with assorted boxes and bags. I sat down on the couch and watched in amazement as Judith made several trips back and forth, filling the room with two complete sets of Passover dishes and pots,

silverware, brand new toys and holiday clothes for my
son and my two little girls, and new clothing and other
items for Simcha and me. I felt like a bride again! Because
we needed everything, it was not hard to accept what she
brought, but nevertheless Simcha and I were speechless
in our gratitude. Because the gifts were anonymous, we
could only thank Judith and her staff for their totally
unexpected gesture!

❀   ❀   ❀

Here it was a week before Pesach and I had been
helplessly watching my husband take care of all the
business of running the house. Pesach cleaning would,
under normal circumstances, have been my number one
priority, for our Sages tell us that we must search for
chametz in every nook and cranny in order to remove
it from our homes. But at our house, there wasn't one
drawer overturned onto the kitchen table, not one curtain
drying on the clothesline, not one piece of furniture being
washed down in the front yard. The kids continued to
run past me with their hands filled with the soon-to-be
forbidden foods — pretzels, crackers, and cookies. As I
overheard my neighbors discussing their latest ideas for
the Seder menu, the pre-Pesach panic which is normal
in the heart of every Jewish housewife set in. I couldn't
believe we hadn't even started! How was Simcha ever
going to singlehandedly finish all the work with only two
days left until Seder night?

The next morning, there was a loud knocking on our
front door. As soon as Simcha opened it, a crowd of single
people from the Yeshiva trooped in. One grabbed a broom,
another a mop, and others reached for assorted bottles
of bleach and cleaning materials. Like happy elves, they
worked through the day and into the evening, scrubbing
the place clean. After all the work was done and they
had left with smiles and good wishes for a happy Pesach,

Simcha took a candle, a feather, and a dustpan and began the traditional search for *chametz*. The children and I listened as Simcha read from the prayerbook the words which declare that any *chametz* which we may still possess should be "as dust." As we saw it, the fact that the house was clean in time for Pesach was nothing short of a miracle.

On Pesach night, as we sat around the table reunited as a family, I read from the Haggadah: *Not only our forefathers did Hashem redeem, but he redeemed us too.*

The light that had shone at the end of my dark tunnel all these months was the belief that Hashem answered my prayers. Although what I experienced was an insignificant moment in world history, nevertheless the Festival of Pesach had great personal significance for me. It marked the beginning of my personal redemption. Even though my healing process would have its setbacks along the way, I had the strong belief that it was Hashem who brought me out from a place of darkness and bondage to a place of light, freedom, and hope for the future.

---

*He has made His wonders to be remembered;
compassionate and merciful is Hashem.*

TEHILLIM 111:4

RIGHT AFTER THE Pesach vacation, I was admitted as an inpatient to Hadassah Mt. Scopus Rehabilitation Center. It is written that Hashem sends the remedy before the affliction. Now everything had come together in its proper time. It turned out that the Director of the Rehabilitation Center, Dr. Megorrah, had consulted with my father-in-law's brother Dr. Arthur (Archie) Abramson in New York when he was establishing his department here. Simcha remembered that when he was a child, Dr. Megorrah had stayed overnight in their apartment in New York. Moreover, Dr. Fast, who was to be in charge of my case, had studied for many years under Dr. Archie. It was amazing to think that both these doctors, who had helped establish the Rehabilitation Unit where I would be a patient for the next year and a half, had such close connections to my husband's family.

There, twice a day, I would be continuing an intensive program of physical and occupational therapy. The fact that I attended these sessions faithfully made me popular with the therapists there. They saw my determination to recover, and it pleased them that I had not given up hope. It all came down to hard work on my part. Rita, the director of the department, was extremely helpful, giving the best of herself, and the therapists tried all sorts of different methods to help me progress. Indeed, most of the time I spent in the Rehabilitation Unit was made pleasant and comfortable because of the wonderful staff.

The goal of the program was that I should learn to function independently in my home. The occupational therapy room was equipped with a real kitchen, where I learned how to carry a pot filled with water, bake a cake, and even cook french fries. I couldn't bear the thought of being dependent on others, and I wanted to be able to do everything for myself. The process was always two steps forward and one step back. Everything was a struggle and at the same time a triumph. Slowly my self-confidence was strengthened along with my abilities until I saw that I would eventually be able to take on the weight of my household jobs again.

On the second day in the Rehabilitation Unit, one of the doctors asked me a question: "What is the most important thing that you want to accomplish here?" After thinking a moment, I answered that I wanted to be able to pin my baby's diapers closed. To me that meant being normal. When I was growing up, the word "normal" meant mediocre, blase, boring — and these things weren't enough for me! "Normal" was definitely not what I wanted to be! I wanted to be different and that meant *more* than okay. Now, however, I realized that just being normal would be the most special gift anyone could ask for.

Walking around in my Jobst suit, I attracted a lot of sympathy. "Don't feel bad for me," I'd want to say whenever I sensed pity. "I'll be just fine, *b'ezrat Hashem.*" I felt very fortunate and happy to be alive. I had lost two joints in little fingers, but I still had all my fingers. I took things day by day, and I didn't have expectations that couldn't be fulfilled. My progress was slow and steady.

Once during a physiotherapy session, a guest appeared and started bombarding me with all kinds of interesting questions. Answering her was such a distraction that my therapist was able to manipulate my body past the pain threshold I had before. "You know, this was the best session we've ever had!" the therapist told me. "Maybe you could arrange to have a guest every day!" From that I learned that distraction is one of the best ways to overcome pain.

It was always a happy time when my children came to visit me in the occupational therapy room. They thought it was funny to see their *Imma* playing children's games, like catching a ball or dressing a doll. I explained to them that I was playing so that I could help my fingers get used to doing things again.

I also enjoyed doing arts and crafts projects, like I had done as a child. Once I made a bamboo lampshade, and another time I wove a decorative table mat. A linoleum line cut became my annual Rosh Hashanah greeting card that I send each year to friends and family. Besides learning how to move and manipulate my fingers again, I had to relearn to experience tactile sensations. The nerve endings at the tips of my fingers had been destroyed in the fire, and touching anything for me was like rubbing raw flesh. The demanding therapy included getting used to feeling different textures again, and doing things like finding buttons hidden inside bowls of sand and rice.

In spite of my progress, I felt helpless, not being able to do much to help my children in their daily lives. I believed, however, that I would eventually be able to, and perhaps even pin diapers all by myself. Ironically, when I finally went home three months later, and was able to use my hands in a limited way, Israeli disposable diapers had just replaced the old cloth diapers and diaper pins became obsolete! What a relief that was, because even though I was physically able to pin a diaper, my hands were still very weak. It would have been quite a project to pin a diaper on a squirming, struggling baby.

❋   ❋   ❋

Before the fire, I could have been described as a harried mother, often late, rarely meeting deadlines, and in a state of frustration a lot of the time. I generally found it more interesting to finish my conversation on the street corner with a friend than to run home in time to make lunch. Those physical chores were always secondary to me — until I got home and had to deal with hungry, tired, and cranky kids. Then I would berate myself: Why didn't I come home earlier and leave time to prepare for this moment! For me, it could have been Yom Kippur every day — immersed in prayer and communicating with Hashem. The Jewish people led by Moshe *Rabbenu*, wandered through the desert for forty years; their clothing never wore out or needed mending; there was no food preparation since manna fell from Heaven; there was little physical effort or daily chores to deal with. Living that life would have been fine with me. The physical demands always seemed to be pulling me away from the spiritual world I longed for — and into a house of frequent turmoil.

In the hospital, with plenty of time to think, I came to the conclusion that I had to make a change in the direction my life had been moving in until then. Life had evolved quickly from being a new bride to finding myself a busy mother of young active children. When a person is in the midst of his life with its daily demands, it is hard to find time to think and reevaluate goals and aspirations. I was thankful that Hashem had given me this time. The process of my personal growth was like that of a butterfly emerging from the cocoon, leaving the old form behind. My previously harried life was no longer, and the butterfly would be my newly directed life as I would create it from now on. I saw clearly that my job now was to integrate the spirituality that I longed for with the reality of my daily life with my family. I realized that the most meaningful spiritual communication would be fulfilled by my being a wife and mother. Was that not what I had fought to live for? It would take time, but I was confident that I would succeed.

❋   ❋   ❋

Judith often came to the Rehabilitation Unit to see me. Once she brought me a large pad of paper and a beautiful set of magic markers, and with gentleness and kindness, she encouraged me to draw — to be creative.

As I took a marker in my hand, I suddenly remembered a photograph of myself — before the fire — helping my daughter Devorah to get dressed. I thought of my hands in that photograph as a woman looks longingly at the portrait of a baby who has died, a lost love, something dear that is gone forever. I mourned for my lost hands, which I had never appreciated enough — the hands with which I had sewn my wedding dress, the hands which had worn my wedding ring, the hands which had held my babies and caressed and comforted them when they cried.

Standing by the window overlooking King David's Tomb, I helped
Devorah get dressed.

Throughout those long, painful months I watched my burned hands change in front of my eyes, to black and blue, then swollen like mitts, and held in slings in front of me. It was not easy for me to forget what my hands once were and what they had become. Would these hands ever function as the "golden hands" they once had been?

I came out of my reverie, grasped the marker firmly, and began to draw. Thank God, I still had the gift of being able to express myself with my hands, and it felt the same — disfigured though they were.

Simcha and I often spoke to Barbara, our social worker, during my months in the Burn Unit. She was genuinely concerned about preparing him for all the ramifications of living with the physical deformity which results from severe burns like mine. A broken leg heals, she emphasized, but scars from a fire last forever. She wanted him to be aware that many marriages end up in divorce when one of the couple is a burn victim.

Simcha reassured her, as he repeatedly reassured me, that this wasn't a problem for us because we loved each other. "I didn't marry Chaya Malka only because of the smoothness of her skin," he told her. "The scars are not intrinsic to our relationship at all." Nevertheless, Simcha and I had benefited from talking with Barbara several times a week. "You need a neutral person to verbalize these things," Simcha confided in me. We were disappointed to be "losing" Barbara when I was transferred as an inpatient to the Rehabilitation Unit on Mount Scopus. She recommended we continue our sessions by talking to the hospital psychologist who treated amputee, stroke and burn victims there.

At first I went alone to our appointments. When I entered his office, I didn't know what to expect — I had never been to a psychologist before. As I sank down into a comfortable chair, waiting for him to arrive, I began to observe things, as I like to do. I noted all the prints of famous artists on the walls, and the various gadgets on his desk. I wondered what we would talk about.

When he arrived, he introduced himself and started off by asking me very direct and embarrassing questions. I tried to explain that the things he thought my husband and I would have difficulty with, did not apply to us. I went back a few times, even though I didn't feel our conversations were getting anywhere. We somehow lacked a common understanding, a common perspective. For the last visit, Simcha came with me and spoke to him alone as well. "I knew right away what he was getting at," Simcha told me later. "I told him about how it says in our sources that real love doesn't depend on the physical. I assured him how much I loved you and how much I wanted you to come home so our family could be complete again."

Baruch Hashem, Simcha and I got through those difficult times together.

I encountered some very sad cases in the Rehabilitation Ward. Shlomo Argov, the highly respected Israeli Ambassador to London, was shot down in cold blood by an Arab terrorist. For days the news of this horrible act dominated the front pages of every newspaper. But, like all "news," eventually his name disappeared from the headlines. What a shock it was, then, to hear that the patient slumped over in his wheelchair was the same Shlomo Argov, a pathetic shadow of his former self. I used to watch as he was wheeled out by an attendant into the hospital garden and taken around the pond for a stroll. My heart went out to him and I prayed that Hashem have mercy on him and his family.

It was very difficult for me to sit at the table across from a certain well-known lawyer whose hands had been badly burned. He was going through the same painful rehabilitation and therapy that I had gone through. His hands looked the way the doctors had warned me my hands would look, if I didn't constantly move them or place them into certain positions. I felt like a bit of an expert on the subject, and since we shared the same therapists, I would ask them questions about his progress and offer advice. Eventually he was fitted for a Jobst suit and gloves like I had been.

❋   ❋   ❋

Shua was almost three years old, and soon he would have his first haircut. Until the age of three, it is a custom to allow a little boy to grow an uncut mane of hair. "Behold, man is like a tree of the field," the Torah tells us (*Devarim* 20:19). Man is compared to a tree for he and the tree both grow from a seed, reach maturity, bear fruit and extend branches! Because of this, many Jewish communities have the custom of symbolically applying to little boys, the Jewish laws pertaining to fruit trees. During the first three years of a tree's life, its fruits are not to be picked, and likewise we let the hair of a boy grow for his first three years. The age of three also represents the beginning of a child's education in Torah and mitzvot. Accordingly, at three, he has an *Upsheren* — his hair is cut, leaving the *payos* (traditional sidelocks), and officially starting him off on the path of Torah. Friends, family, and prominent members of the community each snip off a strand of hair, but leave the main job for the barber. In Israel, many Jews perform this ceremony for all eligible three-year-old boys together in Meron on the day of *Lag ba-Omer.*

I told Simcha that I had always dreamed of taking Shua to Meron for his third-birthday haircutting. How happy I was when we began to make actual plans so that I would be able to fulfill my dream. We would rent a car or a van roomy enough to accommodate my need to move around and have ample leg space.

Simcha, his parents, and our two older children arrived to pick me up from the hospital the day before *Lag ba-Omer* in a rented, air-conditioned car. "How my heart sang as I saw you walking slowly towards us," my mother-in-law, Evelyn, told me later.

We were all in very festive spirits as we drove north up the coast and then through Galilee. We stayed overnight in Safed, in the hotel of a friend of Simcha's family, and we left before sunrise the next morning. We wanted to arrive in Meron in time for the sunrise prayers before the haircutting would begin. Although we were so excited and anxious to reach our destination, we nevertheless had to stop every hour along the road so I could walk around. This constant exercise prevented me from getting stiff. We were among the thousands of people making this annual pilgrimage commemorating the *yahrtzeit* of R. Shimon Bar Yochai, who wrote the mystical *Zohar* during his years of hiding from the Romans. Visiting his grave is also believed to have special healing powers. Ascending the hill to Meron, we drove slowly through crowds of people who were either walking or camping on each side of the road. Seeing me in my rubber mask through the car window, people would run back and forth alongside our car expressing shock. Two people put their faces right up to the closed car window, staring at me in my Jobst suit. "What's this?" they demanded to know. My in-laws were quite upset by such behavior, but I realized it was just insensitive and not malicious. Further up the hill, my father-in-law, Sam, and I got out of the car and started walking.

"Did Simcha ever tell you my brother's story?" he asked.

"Oh, yes," I answered. "Dr. Archie was shot during World War II, and his spine was shattered. Simcha told me they didn't expect him to live."

As we got to the top of the hill, a young man turned his

head to stare. "Mind your own business!" Sam shouted. Then he turned to me and continued. "But Archie survived, and lived to have a distinguished career in medicine although he was confined to a wheelchair." He paused. "Do you know why, Chaya Malka?"

"Why?" I asked.

"Because he was a tough cookie, that's why!" He looked at me and smiled. "It runs in the family, I guess."

The fact is, most people were kind, warm, and understanding when they saw me, and that was why it was particularly shocking for Sam to see others who were not.

＊　　＊　　＊

As I struggled with the scissors to make the first cut of Shua's soft curls, I saw Evelyn turn away. It must have hurt her to see me working so hard to accomplish such a simple task. Sam realized that I just couldn't do it myself, and he gently took my hand and helped me to squeeze the scissors so I could succeed at snipping off those strands of hair.

Lag b'Omer in Meron: I struggled with the scissors to make the first cut of Shua's hair.

Later that same morning, we drove back to Safed. In a park in the center of town we met up with other families from our Yeshiva who had been traveling by rented bus. They had also been to Meron for their sons' first haircut. Yehuda, our friend and official barber, was busy giving real haircuts to the little boys, as our attemps at haircutting at Meron had been less than perfect. Everyone was happy, enjoying the park and eating delicious baked goods that had been prepared for breakfast. That evening in the hotel in Safed, a friend came to help me take off and put back on my Jobst suit. I was so thankful that I wouldn't have to ask my mother-in-law to do this job, since I believed it would have been too painful for her and embarrassing for me. The whole trip was a treat — our accommodations were cozy, and the meals were delicious, and the children were happy — even though the four-hour ride each way was hard for me.

The visit to Meron was one of many brief vacations from the hospital. Over the summer I was often home for Shabbat with my family. I was getting emotionally and physically ready for being home, for making the transition from my final discharge as a permanent patient from the department, to being an outpatient for the next year and a half.

❋ ❋ ❋

PNAI, Parents of North American Israelis, is a wonderful organization in which my parents are active members. It functions as a support group for parents whose children have emigrated to Israel, and helps them cope with the difficulties of life without their children and grandchildren. It also extends help through many available services to the young families in Israel. Some of these dedicated people visited me in the hospital and then afterwards when I returned home. Tobey, the daughter of the vice president of PNAI, came to visit me on her mother's suggestion. We had a lot in common, having grown up in Connecticut and having both attended FIT (Fashion Institute of Technology) in New York. I know she was afraid to see me at first, having never before seen anyone who was burned. It was a natural feeling on her part to doubt that she could offer me anything. From the first, however, we felt like sisters and she comforted me by her presence.

At the Rehabilitation Ward, I was no longer the center of attention as I had been in the Burn Unit. I was with a lot of older patients who had lost limbs, or who were paralyzed from strokes they had suffered. Although I felt that I was the "lucky" one, because I was getting better, still it was hard and painful work. I often felt lonely since I had fewer visitors. Tobey would often come during that period, and spending time with her felt good.

The moment the news of the fire reached them, the PNAI emergency network went into action. The Connecticut chapter started the Malka Fund, with my parents' approval, for collecting money. Because PNAI is not a fund-raising organization, they had to get special permission from the National Board, and after final approval was received, an extensive mailing campaign was organized on our behalf, which brought a wonderful response.

I wrote regularly to PNAI, keeping them updated on my progress. My letters always appeared in the local Connecticut chapter newsletter, *The Bridge*.

Dearest PNAI Members,
   On behalf of my family, I would like to thank you for your prayers, your concern, your generosity, and your strength. This experience has enabled me to feel the oneness of our great nation, Israel. Never before have I been so proud and happy about the greatness of our people. I have cried from joy many times upon receiving your beautiful and warm wishes.
   Baruch Hashem, we are all well. I spend Shabbos and holidays with my family and have started to make the long

journey home. *Baruch Hashem,* I can dance, run, pick up my children, sew a dress, boil an egg, and light Shabbos candles. Every day is a gift. Every child is a gift. I wish we could feel this without the pain of losing it first.

Thank you very much.

Devorah, Shua, and Esther, Chaya Malka and Simcha

How happy I felt the first time I was able to mend a torn dress by myself.

The beauty of Mount Zion has a dreamlike quality, and before the fire I had loved living there, despite the hardships. Even when we finally had a "normal" apartment in the Jewish Quarter — an apartment with smooth walls, and real doors for the bedrooms — I longed for the special beauty of Mount Zion. My prayer remained that some day we would return.

As a result of the many generous donations received and the various appeals made to the Jewish community both in Israel and abroad, we were able to consider buying our own apartment in any neighborhood we chose. But the advantages of buying an apartment anywhere else were outweighed by the opportunity to stay on Mount Zion in the small apartment we were given by Rabbi Goldstein. The neighbors, who were also close friends, knew I would continue to need help in the coming years. Their willingness to give it unconditionally, day in and day out, at all hours of the day or night, was a quality of the extraordinary *chesed* offered to me. Being so dependent on others is hard, yet the manner in which my neighbors made themselves available whenever help was needed was always one of cheerfulness, respect, and support, and they made me feel that whatever they were doing, it was no big deal.

Sometimes it is said that today there are no righteous ones left for us to emulate. But I think that it is possible to look for that special quality in other people, with which each Jew is born, and train ourselves to see how good it is, to emulate it, and become enriched. I certainly saw how righteous our community was. And after having received so much *chesed*, the desire to want to pay it back was and still is overwhelming. I will probably feel indebted for the rest of my life. Rabbi Goldstein taught us that it is the proper thing to feel the need to repay a *chesed*, because the world runs on the law of measure for measure (*middah k'neged middah*). I used to worry about how I would ever be able to pay back all the *chesed* that was done for me. I felt in a very unbalanced position, and yet I had to go on with my everyday life. How could I repay my debt to someone for taking care of my baby for eight months? That's a lot of diapers changed, baths given, meals fed, a lot of love provided. But I learned that if a person does an act of *chesed* for another, then an act of *chesed* will be done for him in turn. Sometimes it will be repaid through another person at another time. Once friends went to the States for three weeks and asked me to watch their child. I was thrilled, and I felt grateful to Hashem that He let me repay one drop in the bucket. After all, it was only for three weeks — not for eight months. If ever a friend's clothes dryer would break down on a rainy day, and she would show up at my door with wet laundry, I would jump at the chance to repay my overdraft. But there would still be times when I would run out of milk and have to borrow from my neighbors. I could never say, I'm only going to give from now on and not receive. I have a picture on my wall that helps me to remember the significance of giving and receiving. In it, two hands are grasping a bouquet of flowers, and it is impossible to tell which hand is giving the flowers and which hand is receiving them. If I looked at it long enough, it seemed to switch back and forth. Now I understand that sometimes I will be on the receiving end too. I call it the *chesed* circle.

Hashem is my strength and my shield;
my heart trusted in Him, and I am helped.
Therefore my heart greatly rejoices,
and with my song I will praise him.

TEHILLIM 28:7

AFTER TWO MONTHS as an inpatient at the Rehabilitation Center, the doctors decided I could continue my therapy while living at home. During the late-summer heat, I would leave my apartment every day wearing my Jobst suit and mask, hurry into a waiting cab, and travel to the clinic on Mount Scopus. The ride in the sweltering taxi was only bearable because I knew that soon I would be comfortable again in the air-conditioned hospital. After a long morning of physiotherapy I returned home, hot and exhausted. I would lie down for half an hour just to cool off in my room, which had air conditioning newly installed just for me.

At first, I was afraid to be left alone and I had daily help in the house. Once I awoke in the middle of the night to find that Devorah had partly slipped through the guard-rail of her top bunk. I could not believe my eyes when I saw her hanging in mid-air yet sleeping soundly, her head wedged between the mattress and the rail. There was nothing that I could do to help her since I did not have the strength to pull her through to safety. I woke Simcha up, feeling helpless and incapable.

My life at home before the fire had been so busy, so full. Now that I was home for good, I felt handicapped because I couldn't do the things I used to do. I began to realize something else too. The long road ahead was filled with doubt and insecurity about whether I would be able to discipline and handle my children.

Once I was sitting in a chair in our family room, and the kids were running around me. Shua and Devorah were hard to catch — they eluded my grip. They did not want to be held for more than a few seconds at the most. I must have wanted them to do something that they didn't want to do, like washing their hands after using the bathroom, or listening to one of my long educational lectures.

The physical reality was so overwhelming, that I had to make choices between giving them spiritual training and teaching them more practical things like brushing their teeth regularly. I wanted to give them all the skills that they would need for a lifetime, but I lacked the means and I had unrealistic expectations of them.

There was a lot to overcome. They had been spoiled by doting grandparents and a whole community of concerned friends who wanted to make them happy. In addition to my physical handicap, I also lacked the ability to get them back in line and listening to their mother. I was trying so hard to make up for lost time. I felt that catching them was like trying to catch a slippery fish.

As soon as I was home for good, I wanted to bring Esther home too. My friend Sarah reassured me that there was no hurry. "Take your time, Chaya Malka. You need time to readjust to being home before you take on the added responsibility of a toddler. Look, we're in constant touch with each other. You can see her every day. But we'll be happy to have her as long as there is a need. Don't worry." I realized that Sarah was right. As much as I wanted my baby home, I knew it was unrealistic to think I could assume full care of her now. And *baruch Hashem*, she was happy where she was.

After a while, we started taking Esther home for lunch.

Since she attended nursery school on Mount Zion, Simcha would pick her up and bring her home for the afternoon. I already had a housekeeper who came in every day to give the kids lunch. It seemed like a good time to get Esther slowly used to being back with our family. After the meal, Simcha would take her back to the Jewish Quarter. It was a transitional period for all of us. Eventually I realized, though, that the job of a mother is to be responsible for her child's care even when it is difficult. It might be years, I told myself, before it would be easy — but we couldn't wait for the perfect time. I was torn between the desire to take my responsibilities back, and the doubt over whether I could handle them.

When I was growing up, my family used to say "Life isn't always just a bowl of cherries," and one day I told Simcha this and said: "Let's just jump in and start over." I suggested to Sarah that we have an informal party for all the kids, to ease the transition of moving Esther from their house to ours. Sarah thought it was a good idea. We arranged the party to be at a time when all our kids would be around to watch their fathers take down Esther's crib in the Jewish Quarter and put it up again in Esther's room on Mount Zion. As the two men reassembled the crib again in our house, Sarah and I completed the finishing touches at the table before starting the meal. The mood was happy as we all sat down together, and Sarah shared stories with us of Esther's eight-month stay with their family.

Neither of our families wanted the party to be over. Saying goodbye meant that this chapter in our lives had come to an end. As Simcha and I walked our guests out the door, I took Sarah aside. I became quiet, immersed in thought, and she too remained silent. After a short while, I broke the silence, taking her hand in mine. "There is something I want you to know," I told her. "There are no words to express our thanks for the kindness you extended to Esther. I will always be indebted to you, Sarah."

The transition seemed to go easily but sometimes when we were walking down their street in the Jewish Quarter, Esther would break away and toddle over to her old "home." As the months passed, though, she became used to our family again and she knew that her home was with us.

❈   ❈   ❈

My parents remained in close contact with us on the phone, but it was heartbreaking for them to be so far away just when I had come home. My mother could not travel since she had just undergone back surgery, but they decided that my father would come alone to Israel to see how I was doing. They could not believe that I had been discharged from the hospital so soon. We told Dad to come and see for himself so he could bring a good report back to Mom.

Miriam and I enjoyed our father's company as we dined at one of Jerusalem's best Italian restaurants. The summer night air was cool and the sky was starry; the scent of garden flowers mingled with the tantalizing aromas of the different dishes the waiter had placed on our red checkered tablecloth. It was a different atmosphere and a refreshing change from the hospital and being home, and I appreciated the pleasant contrast. I was wearing my mask and straw hat as I always did, but after a while I felt awkward wearing the mask in front of Dad, and I slipped out to the ladies' room where I removed it. Standing there I looked at my eyes looking back at me in the mirror. "That's really you, Malka," I whispered to myself, staring. "There's no question about it." My eyes were unchanged, but my face looked a bit different. It was more red, mainly on the left side, and somewhat scarred and swollen in places. I stared as one might stare

at oneself after having gotten a very short haircut — a
new look — and then I smiled and felt happy, thanking
Hashem that all my features were visible and functioning.

Back at the table, I sat down and Dad began to speak,
"You have remarkable courage, Shelly," he said, using
my childhood nickname. "Not everybody could beat that,"
he suddenly added. Dad also commented on how nice
I looked. He was proud of me. I was thrilled that he
would be able to go home with a good report on my
improvement. One of my most cherished moments of the
evening was being able to pour my father a glass of water
at the table. Time stretched as the water flowed from the
pitcher into his cup. My mind registered those seconds that
I'd be able to fulfill this commandment of honoring my
father, and in general to be able, with Hashem's kindness,
to help others. How grateful I felt. The light had begun to
shine. I didn't allow myself to worry too much about how
my hands would function. I was confident and my heart
was happy.

❊   ❊   ❊

Simcha and I asked ourselves whether or not our situation called for professional help for the children's possible
anger, questions, anxieties, fears about their abrupt and
continued separation from me. We concluded, finally, that
the situation did not call for it. The children seemed to
be accepting reality, surrounded as they were by loving
adults, by their family, and by their peers. They showed no
signs of anxiety — no nightmares or regressive behavior
— so we decided against psychological help.

Evelyn had told me a lot about how the children were
when she and Sam had taken care of them when I was
in the hospital. Simcha would bring Devorah and Shua
to them every day after nursery school, and that was
the arrangement from the day after the fire until I came
home. "They were so wonderful, and we loved taking care

of them," she told me. After the winter was over and the weather got warmer, they took walks together. Devorah never talked about the fire, but if Shua saw a burned stick, he would throw a rock at it, Evelyn told me. For a long while afterwards, whenever he saw a bonfire, or ruins, or anything a little burnt, he would throw stones at it. Sam always let him do it. He'd say, "Hey, Shua, here's another rock — throw!" Once Sam had found Shua looking very angry. He encouraged him to smash some boards for a while, and after a while Shua stopped, feeling better. Later on Sam had talks with Devorah. She would cry to her grandfather, asking if we would ever be all together as a family again. He always reassured her: "Yes, yes, of course you will!"

I myself saw the kids sometimes playing a favorite game: "Fire." I would watch in amazement as they took blankets, threw them on the floor, jumped up and down and covered themselves with them. It was an exciting game for them, trying to reenact what had happened. As time went by, and I observed my children acting out different life situations, whether sad or joyous, I understood that "Fire," like the other games they played, was an important part of growing from life's experiences.

❋   ❋   ❋

One day, while walking past a shoe store on Ben Yehudah Street, in my Jobst suit and face mask, I heard a child cry out to his mother, "Look, look, Imma! There's a clown!" Then I heard the mother say, as I passed them by, "Where? I don't see one." I knew he was talking about me, and underneath my expressionless elastic pressure mask I smiled, because many of my other encounters with people were much more negative. Sometimes, when I walked into stores, both customers and salespeople became suspicious and hostile. "Why are you wearing that?" "Who are you?" They were frightened by the way I looked. When I tried to explain who I was and why I was dressed in this strange attire, they would actually react with disbelief. It was as if they didn't have the patience to hear the truth. They just wanted to get rid of me. At times they wouldn't even accept my money when I wanted to pay for the item I'd come in to purchase.

Children on the street would sometimes shout crude remarks about my appearance. They knew, I think, that there was a sick person underneath what they perceived as a hideous mask, but they reacted only to my weird appearance. I supposed they could not behave otherwise, and because of it I felt sorry for them. No matter how much I could understand it, though, I had to be strong emotionally to withstand the insults and insensitivity. And I was strong; the desire to lead a normal life forced me to get back into things, as I would normally have done if I had no mask on at all. I refused to be a hermit.

Ever since I had become religious at the Yeshiva, I gained a new dimension of self-worth, and this stood me in good stead now. By learning about the relationship that the Creator of the universe has with every person, and how He loves all his creations, how every person is special with something specific to give, I developed the strength to stand up to many difficult situations. Thus, I could throw myself into a situation where people would be repulsed by my appearance, and know that it was the mask they were frightened of, and not the real me underneath. For my essential self was whole and unchanged. I knew who I was.

Even without the mask, I still had to deal with my ugly scars and blotchy red skin. In reality I knew I did not look so nice, but interestingly, nobody I really cared for, not even under insistent prodding, would ever admit it. I am a person who wants to hear the truth, and yet my husband's answer to my questions about my appearance was always the same: "No, you're not ugly. You're my wife,

Chaya Malka, and you are beautiful."

❅   ❅   ❅

The cool air of that first autumn enabled me to take walks to the Jewish Quarter to attend classes or to visit friends. When I did go, I didn't hide. I didn't want people to forget what had happened. It was part of Hashem's Master Plan that it had happened here, affecting so many people.

Revisiting Chabad Street
in the Jewish Quarter.

The residents were not the only ones who suffered. One can only begin to imagine how the firefighters felt when they could not get through the narrow Old City alleyways in their vehicles. Conventional fire engines were just too big to turn the corners of the ancient, winding streets, and get up and down the many stone steps. I read later in a magazine article, how demoralized the firefighters were. They knew it should not have been that way, that they should have been there at the scene of the fire in time to help me and my family. Determined never to let this happen again, soon afterwards they set up a committee to discuss and assess their disturbing experience. One of the firemen pointed out that the Jerusalem sanitation department had an unusual cleaning machine, a small truck able to maneuver the narrow corners and stone steps of the Jewish Quarter. The committee contacted the company in Germany that produced this vehicle, and ordered a fire engine that was smaller and more versatile than standard fire engines on the market. A designer from the German firm came to Jerusalem and he worked with the Fire Department to create the perfect fire engine for the Old City. When the design was in its advanced stages, the company invited the Jerusalem firefighters to Germany to finalize the product. The incredible new vehicle was named "the Trenkle." Once the new vehicle had arrived, the Fire Department realized that in addition to being suited to the Old City, it would also be effective in fighting forest fires amid rows of young saplings. *Baruch Hashem*, the Trenkle has been put to good use in its planned and unplanned role. Its creation was one of the many benefits that came out of our experience.

❋   ❋   ❋

Simcha, the kids, and I visit the Trenkle which is stationed in the Jewish Quarter.

In 1982 the Israeli Army entered Lebanon in order to push back the terrorist bases of the PLO. Israeli soldiers fought fierce battles with the retreating Arab terrorists. Among the war casualties were many young solidiers who were in Burn Units of Israel's major hospitals. Simcha and I wanted to do something to help, and we decided that our example could bring hope and comfort to the burned soldiers and their families.

When Clara answered the phone of the Hadassah Burn Unit, she was very excited to hear my voice. We had a lively conversation, and I filled her in on how I was feeling, how the children were, and plans for the future. Caught up in her enthusiasm, I almost forgot the purpose of my call. When I told her, she understood our concern and appreciated our desire to help but she gently explained that it was too early to talk to these soldiers, because of their serious condition. Following her instructions, we waited a week and tried again. This time we set a date for visiting the injured solidiers.

The day came, and as we drove that familiar road up to the hospital, it suddenly dawned on me that perhaps I was not emotionally prepared to visit these seriously burned soldiers after all. I asked Simcha what he thought. Did *he* feel prepared?

"One can never be prepared for something like this," he replied quietly. I realized he was right. Knowing myself, I spent a few seconds in prayer, asking Hashem for assistance that our mission would be successful.

At first, when we went from bed to bed, at the Burn Unit, I found that it was not always easy for me to express myself. I would enter the room feeling brave and inspired, but after the initial shock of seeing the young soldiers lying there all bandaged up, I sometimes lost my nerve and broke down and start crying. It was very hard to see their suffering, since I knew exactly what they were going through. I was embarrassed, standing there crying when I was supposed to be strong. I learned, after the first few visits, to always walk into the room smiling and let Simcha start the conversation.

Visiting the soldiers was only the beginning of the many visits that Simcha and I made to burn victims. Some were victims of terrible accidents in the home, others of Arab terrorism, such as the Moses family, when a firebomb was thrown at their car. Mrs. Moses and one son died of their burns, and Mr. Moses and his eight-year-old son were badly burned. The other children in the car also suffered injuries. The father of the family was in a lot of pain when we went to visit him at Tel Hashomer Hospital. We entered his room together, and Simcha introduced me. "This is Chaya Malka," he said. "She was once burned very badly. Hashem helped her as He will help you to recover also. You must have strength and courage because there will be a lot of pain, but you will come out of it." Mr. Moses reacted positively and managed to thank us for visiting. This man did survive that great tragedy.

Simcha and I hoped that by serving as an example, it would strengthen each patient's resolve. Despite Hadassah's advanced methods of treating burn victims, I was given an "optimistic" ten percent chance of survival by the doctors who treated me. Even the non-religious doctors admitted that along with faith in Hashem, my determination to survive for the sake of my family sustained me against tremendous odds throughout the torturous and difficult recovery.

"I went through what you are going through," I would say simply, "and I passed through it, *baruch Hashem*." Simcha would add, "We are not saying it is going to be easy, but we got through it together."

One woman I visited had been burned when she had used her own body to put out a fire that was about to spread to a nearby gas balloon. She was afraid the possible explosion would spread throughout the neighborhood, destroying apartments with their families inside. As I walked in, I wondered which words I could offer her, but I had barely introduced myself when Rivka started to tell me her story. To tell the truth, I could not understand every word of her rapid Hebrew, but the intensity in her eyes echoed her words and overwhelmed me. I listened in awe as she spoke of her love of Hashem and of *Am Yisrael,* and how she had never taken money for her services as a healer of ailing women. I realized quickly that Rivka did not need my encouragement at all! She was directing *me* to be strong and at the same time telling herself. She was giving me the inspiration I tried to give others.

One day, on our way back from visiting soldiers, we stopped off at Professor Wexler's clinic for a quick hello. When he came out of his office to call his next patient, he caught sight of us and whisked us enthusiastically past a waiting room full of people. We exchanged warm greetings and before I knew it, he had his camera pointed at me and was ready to click the shutter — he had kept a photographic journal of my case over the last year and a half. He quickly directed me, telling me where to stand and how to hold my hands. Afterwards I took the opportunity to ask his professional opinion: Would I need plastic surgery on my burned outer ear where the cartilage had collapsed? With today's modern medicine, I did not think it would be a complicated procedure to reconstruct it through surgery. Taking a quick look under my wig, he responded, "You're lucky — this wig or any headscarf can serve a dual function." It wasn't such a simple operation after all and since my ear was covered nearly all the time, additional surgery seemed unnecessary to him. I was relieved by his professional opinion. Professor Wexler was proud of my recovery. Whenever I dropped by the Burn Unit after visiting soldiers or other patients, he and the nurses who had cared for me would take the opportunity to introduce me to the new doctors and nurses in the

Ward. I found it very embarrassing to be described as their legendary patient, so I would just smile politely.

❋   ❋   ❋

In spite of my vigorous exercise routine for preventing contraction of the skin, I had to undergo minor knee and hand surgery about a year after I was released from the hospital. The doctors were able to offer me a wider range of movement and mobility with a special surgical technique. Some time after the operation, while the hand had healed very nicely, the site of the knee surgery still remained an open wound. By this time I had a sense of how healing skin should look, so I went to see Professor Wexler. "You're right," he agreed. "It doesn't look so good." My heart sank. During my long hospital stay I had heard of burn wounds which would not heal, and I had overheard the nurses telling a distraught patient about the possibility that he might be changing bandages for the rest of his life. Thus I was very concerned that, God forbid, this could be happening to me. Professor Wexler reminded me of all the major obstacles I had confronted and overcome, and said that he was confident these wounds would heal as the others had. After many months of waiting patiently, his prediction proved correct.

❋   ❋   ❋

Suzy was on the phone, calling from *Kolbotek*, the renowned Israeli Expose TV program. "We're interested in your story," she said, "and we'd like to set a time to come and interview you for the program." I agreed quickly, and before I knew it, the day came when the camera crew was setting up their equipment a few yards away from my front door. It suddenly occurred to me that the point of the interview was unclear to me. What angle were they interested in? I knew I had a great opportunity to make known the miracle that had occurred, and I didn't want the emphasis of the interview to be on any other subject. I began to feel anxious and worried that I might be put on the spot and say the wrong thing. I asked one of my neighbors to act as an intermediary between the interviewer and me, and after a quick conference on the side, I was reassured by the interviewer that he would let me express myself fully and stress what I wanted to stress. At the same time he would also alert the public to the dangers of gas heating. Natural gas has an excellent safety record when it is used properly, but one has to be aware of safety precautions and the possibility of gas leaks.

I was very nervous as the filming began, as I was not used to public speaking. But I made myself imagine the interview as a personal conversation, and I was able to ignore the cameras and assorted media paraphernalia. I tried to communicate my own ideas and concepts about my experience and its spiritual ramifications.

❈   ❈   ❈

Ten years later, as I stood in line in a large supermarket in Jerusalem, the young man who was packing my groceries suddenly asked, "Weren't you on *Kolbotek* a few years ago?" Although I replied calmly that indeed I was, I was amazed! At the time I was interviewed, I was "disguised" in my Jobst suit and mask, and now I was dressed as any Jerusalem housewife would be. How could he have recognized me after ten years? I understood then how great an impression the interview had made on the public.

❈   ❈   ❈

Chanukah is a special time for remembering miracles. Twenty three hundred years ago, the Maccabees, a small group of pious Jews, fought against the powerful Hellenist-Syrian forces to regain the Temple that stood defiled in

Jerusalem. When the Jews prevailed and vanquished their enemies, they searched and found only one remaining container of pure olive oil with the High Priest's seal. Although there was only enough oil to burn for one day, they lit the menorah and, miraculously, the oil burned for eight days.

In our family, like Jewish families everywhere, we light Chanukah candles to commemorate that miracle, eat traditional pancakes fried in oil, and retell the Chanukah story to our children. But we add our personal commemoration: We want our children to realize that the God of Israel Who made the miracle for the Jewish Nation, so many years ago, performed a miracle for me, their mother, and for our family during this time. To mark the special significance this holiday has for our family, we hand-decorate a colorful poster which we hang above our Chanukah menorah.

On Chanukah, outside the Land of Israel, Jews say, "*Nes gadol hayah sham* — A great miracle happened there." Here in Israel, we say, "*Nes gadol hayah po* — A great miracle happened *here!*"

*... You Who lift me up from the gates of death,
that I may tell all your praises in the gates of
the daughters of Zion.
I will rejoice in your salvation.*

TEHILLIM 9:14-15

 IT IS WRITTEN IN the book *Chayei Adam* that a person for whom a miracle has occurred may commemorate the day of the miracle in the succeeding years. This applies to the person himself, to whom the miracle has occurred, as well as to his or her progeny. In describing a great fire from which he and his family were saved in Vilna in the year 1803, the author recounts the destruction and injury that resulted from that great calamity, and adds:

> Hashem in His compassion and mercy left us all among the living. Even though I suffered great monetary loss, the money was taken instead of our lives. And in order to recount the wonders of Hashem, as it is written, "He made a memorial for his wonders, compassionate and merciful is Hashem" (*Tehillim* 111:4). I have accepted upon myself and my children that the day of the fifteenth of Kislev will be a day of fasting and repentance, and at night we will gather and light *Yom Tov* lights and recite songs of praise to Hashem, after which will follow a festive celebration.

The first anniversary of the fire was quickly approaching. I was reunited with my family, running my home, and on the road to recovery. Simcha and I decided it would be appropriate for me to invite all the women who had helped me throughout the year, to a festive meal in honor of the miracle that had occurred.

I was thrilled to hear that my mother would be coming to stay with me and the kids while Simcha was away on business in the States. I knew it was a real sacrifice for her to leave Dad at home, but appreciating how I would benefit from being under my mother's care during this period, they agreed that she would come without him. It was at the end of her stay with us that we planned the festive brunch to commemorate our miracle. Mom and Evelyn, my mother-in-law, who was also in Israel at the time, were indispensable in helping to make it a success, as were my friends, who each prepared food for the festive meal.

When the day came, my mother and mother-in-law helped arrange the house and set the table. Everything was laid out beautifully, and as the women arrived they placed their decorated cakes, fresh salads, and hors d'oeuvres on the table. The colorful flowers and beautifully arranged platters added to the festivity.

Miriam, Mom, and I with some of our children before the brunch commemorating the miracle.

As I sat down at the beautiful table, surrounded by the women who had prayed for me, helped me, and loved me, tears welled up inside me. This was a day in which an entire box of tissues would be used up to wipe away my tears. Deep emotions filled the room as we sat there together, talking straight from our hearts. It was a day in which my friends and family rejoiced together and shared my triumph. Even though I was wearing my mask and still had a long way to go on the road to complete recovery, everyone knew how far I had come. It was a tremendous feeling of relief. We had struggled through most difficult times and had prevailed. These were precious moments we would want to remember, and everyone wanted to say something to express her feelings.

One of my friends expressed what many people feel when they become newly religious — the thought that the Master of the Universe, Who loves and cares for us, would never let anything bad happen to us or our loved ones. She was talking about how the bubble bursts with the realization that serving God does not mean that nothing painful will ever happen. I remember her words especially because they were so shockingly true and real. She read aloud from *Tehillim* 112:7 where it says of the righteous person, "of evil tidings he will have no fear, his heart is firm, confident in Hashem." Misfortune comes even to the most righteous of men, and no one is immune to tragedy and suffering.

Rebbetzin Goldstein, the wife of our Rabbi, had always taught us Jewish concepts in a fresh and exciting way. Over many years in the Women's Division of the Yeshiva, where she guided and inspired us, she was always able to demonstrate clearly that what the Torah says is right. She taught us to let go of our old ideas and preconceptions and accept what is written in our holy sources. She was very aware of wordly affairs and was able to show us the fallacies of today's attitudes when compared to the eternal values of the Torah. The Rebbetzin had always said that even though everyone has problems in life, the difference is how a religious person handles them.

Now, when it was her turn to speak, she quoted the Chazon Ish in the name of the Baal Shem Tov: "The Baal Shem Tov, of blessed memory, says that when Hashem wants to punish man, He takes away his faith. When a person has no faith, he suffers greatly. A person cannot live a completely happy life without it. I think it's much easier to be a religious person because then it is possible to understand things much more easily." Then she added a very personal note. "When we lost our baby several years ago, it was very difficult. I cried a lot — it was such a sudden thing, a crib death. They don't know why it happens — a perfectly healthy baby! They're doing a lot of research on it today. Afterwards the doctors suggested I speak to a social worker or a psychologist, but I told them I didn't need it. I knew the baby's death was from Hashem and I totally accept Hashem's ways.

"When you have *bitachon*, trust and confidence, you know that whatever happens is God's will. I've heard how in non-religious homes such a tragedy can break up a marriage... The Chazon Ish says that faith is the belief that there is no such thing as coincidence, that, everything that happens under the sun is *hashgachah pratit*, Divine Providence.

"When the fire broke out," she went on, "the true reason was not that the pipes were filled with air, or because of spontaneous combustion, or anything else like that. It happened because it was decreed by Hashem — and that's that!

"Now, it's easy to say, 'Have faith,' as long as things are going well. The *real* test of faith is when things are hard. Not only did Chaya Malka have faith in Hashem at the time of the explosion, but afterwards she trusted in Hashem, all during the painful ordeal of her recovery.

She didn't talk — she *did*. Words are cheap but action is hard work, and act she did. Thank you, Chaya Malka," she concluded. "You've shown us all how the soul of a Jewish woman can reach great spiritual heights. May our children and grandchildren emulate your deeds." As she sat down beside me, everyone applauded her profound and meaningful speech.

Miriam, my sister, rose to speak next. "When I see you, Chaya Malka, I think of all the difficulties you have had to face. From the time I heard that there had been a terrible fire in the Jewish Quarter and you had been badly hurt, I don't even know how I kept *myself* together. Nothing like this had ever happened to our family before.

"It took a long time for the reality of the situation to hit me. I remember pacing the floor in the emergency waiting room alone, frantically reciting *Tehillim* and crying, crying and praying to Hashem. I realized that I would have to muster up all the *emunah*, all the faith that was within me. I really put all my eggs in one basket. 'Okay, Miriam,' I told myself. 'It's time to pray with all the strength that has always been there within you, dormant and untapped.' I also felt that it didn't matter how much I would have to do, or the endless amount of energy it would take, that I always knew that it was a gift that Hashem had made me strong. And yet I perceive you, Chaya Malka, as a veritable tower of strength. Physically you were always more fragile than I was; your strength was in your spirit and your unswerving belief. Ever since we became religious, I saw how you developed your tremendous spiritual stamina. In this area, you helped me a lot although you were not aware of it. There you were, fighting for your life, and it was primarily your *emunah* working for you. We saw how you pulled yourself out of the grip of death. And looking back to the day of the fire, that total devastation, the shock of everyone around, it is truly a miracle that we are all here together today."

Miriam turned and gave me a big hug. As we stood there embracing, my mother and Evelyn stood up and joined us. But when we sat down, Miriam had more to say. She turned to the women in the room. "I think my sister and I are closer now, and are able to share things as we never did before. I went through a frightening time during a recent pregnancy, and I was able to handle it because of my sister and the strength of her belief and trust in Hashem, her conviction that Hashem is the only One who gives life and takes life away. At first as I faced this personal crisis, I did not know where to turn. I worried constantly, but in the end it was Chaya Malka's example that showed me the way. I kept thinking, Hashem will not test me unless I can handle it, and eventually I found the strength to cope with my fears. My sister has been an inspiration to me and to the people around her in our community."

I thanked Miriam for her heartfelt words as I wiped more tears from my cheeks. Then another woman rose to speak. She recalled the feelings in the Yeshiva during the period right after the fire. "For two weeks, every Monday and Thursday, everyone except pregnant or nursing women fasted. It was like Yom Kippur for days. Besides the fasting, we all sat together with the Rabbi in the Study Hall making different resolutions in our lives. We felt emotionally and spiritually that Chaya Malka's recovery was our responsibility. The *achdut* — the feeling of togetherness — was tremendous. We would stay up till past midnight every night," she recounted. "Nobody could rest. We kept asking ourselves why this had happened to us. Our hearts were being scrubbed out. We had to do *teshuvah* for our own deeds and we believed that the merit of our *teshuvah* would help Chaya Malka recover."

When the speeches were finished, all eyes turned in my direction. There was so much going on inside of me, and in anticipation of this anniversary, I wanted to bring all these deep feelings to the surface and express them to my friends. As the Rebbetzin had taught us to always quote from source material, in anticipation of this day, I had studied various books to help me articulate some of the ideas that I wanted to express. I opened the *Meshech Chochmah* written by the saintly Rabbi Meir Simcha of Dvinsk, known as the *Or Same'ach*, and began my prepared speech.

"The Or Same'ach states, 'Hashem brings suffering upon man with a distinct purpose. He is educating us, making us realize our errors, striking us as a father strikes his son. Hashem is not like a master who disregards the welfare of his slave, inevitably leading to his suffering; rather, He intentionally brings suffering upon man. Thus the Jews err when they say, Because Hashem is not with us, we suffer. Hashem is hidden from us only when we do not recognize that everything He does is really for the best.'

"This is what the prophet Hoshea meant when he said, 'O Yisrael, return to Hashem your God, for you have stumbled in your iniquity' (*Hoshea* 14:2)... Recognize that suffering is His way of rousing you to repent and healing the sickness of sin."

I paused as I looked at my audience. My heart was full and I wanted to express my appreciation and give thanks to all those women who shared this very special occasion. We reached this day together recognizing that our prayers had been heard and our hopes realized. It is written that whoever works for the Shabbat, delights in the Shabbat. So here was the core of people who had worked together and here we were delighting in the fruits of our labor. The most vital thing that I wanted to express weighed so heavily on my heart that I just broke down crying at this point and gave up any hope of continuing my speech. These were the words I left unsaid:

Having felt the great honor of being given back the most
challenging and precious job of being a wife to my hus-
band and a mother to my children, I want to tell you all,
my friends, what a privilege it is to be given the opportunity
to do this job, of caring for our families. Please give it its
proper honor and treasure it always! We grow from our tests
and trials into better and stronger Jews with greater faith in
Hashem. Who knew how things would turn out? Now that
a year has passed and I am emotionally healthy, I have not
become a hermit, I am not afraid of my scars, I sigh with
relief that the worst is over. If I had worried about how I
would look, about whether I could ever have more children,
whether my husband and children would shy away from
me with my new appearance, then I surely would have
given up hope or lost my mind. I took each day as it came,
and baruch Hashem, things worked out for the best.

The first year we decided to celebrate the miracle
with my friends, but in subsequent years, as the children
became old enough to understand, we have followed
more closely to the words of the Chayei Adam. We dress
in our holiday clothes and have a nighttime festive meal
together. These are cherished moments when, during the
meal, Simcha and I take turns telling the story of the
miracle of the fire to the children. The next morning we
wake up before sunrise and excitedly prepare to walk to
the Western Wall. The horizon is always glowing orange as
we approach the Kotel for early morning prayers. There
are many appropriate *Tehillim* which we say throughout
the day. After the prayer service is over, we give charity
to the poor people there and distribute sweets among the
men and women worshipers with whom we pray. If they
inquire as to the reason for the goodies, we happily tell
them our story. After everyone wishes us well, we proceed
to Ararat Street, the site of the fire, where Devorah, Shua,
Esther, and I recite the blessing, "Blessed are You, King of
the Universe, Who made a miracle for me in this place."

Our other children, who were born after the fire, and all their descendants after them, will continue to say the same blessing, God willing, only concluding, "Who made a miracle for my mother (or grandmother) in this place." Later, back at home, we share a special breakfast and the children go to school. Because of their festive appearance, their peers inquire as to the reason, and then they get a chance to tell their friends and teachers their story of this special day. A day for kindness, repentance, and charity.

Every year I recite a blessing at the site of the fire on Ararat Street.

The children of Your servants shall continue,
and their seed shall be established before You.

TEHILLIM 102:29

Epilogue

IT HAS BEEN FOURTEEN YEARS since that eventful day that changed my life and the life of my friends and family.

Even now, I still speak of the events in my life as having happened "before the fire" or "after the fire." The strong smell of gas still causes me to feel anxiety. But as the trauma of the fire fades more and more into the past, the feelings that remain are those of overwhelming gratitude to Hashem. He has returned my life and fulfilled my prayers to be a wife to my husband and a mother to my children.

We say in the Shabbat morning prayers, "We still cannot sufficiently thank You, Hashem, for even one of the thousand thousand, thousands of thousands and myriad myriads of favors that You performed for our ancestors and for us." I can never sufficiently thank Hashem. To all my family and friends and all those unknown Jewish souls who helped me with their prayers across the world, I offer my gratitude.

I am still called by the hospital to visit burn victims and their families. I consider it an honor to show them that with strength and confidence the soul of man can triumph over the greatest physical challenges.

I had always hoped to have a large family — "a family blessed with children," as we say in Hebrew. As I lay recovering from my burns during those weeks and months, however, it occurred to me that I might not be able to have any more children. I had to ultimately come to terms with the fact that such decisions — like everything else in our lives — are up to Hashem, and not in our hands.

What a joy and a comfort it was then when our daughter Yael was born just two years after the fire. Like her sisters Devorah and Esther, Yael is named after a great woman in Jewish history. With her birth, I felt that Hashem had given us a new beginning.

Baruch Hashem, our family has continued to grow in our home on Mount Zion. I have regained almost all of my abilities and have been able to continue my art work, sewing, and haircutting.

Simcha has received his Rabbinical ordination and now teaches in a program for post-high-school boys from abroad at Yeshiva Toras Yisrael. Simcha went back to the States recently for the "Original Diaspora Yeshiva Band Gala Reunion" in Carnegie Hall. Over three thousand enthusiastic fans attended.

Devorah is attending a women's college; Esther is a successful student at Bais Yaakov High School; Shua learns at a Yeshiva in Jerusalem; Yael is already Bat Mitzvah; the younger children are in primary and nursery school; and we were blessed for the new year with a new baby who was born on Erev Rosh Hashanah this year.

Miriam and her family now live on Yishuv Metzad, the Yeshiva's settlement in the Judean Hills.

On this past Yom Kippur, as is our custom, the Yeshiva Community *daven*ed at King David's Tomb. I listened along with the rest of the congregation as the *chazan* began to intone the sacred *U'netaneh Tokef* prayer:

> On Rosh Hashanah you will be written, and on Yom Kippur you will be sealed. How many will pass from the earth and how many will be created? Who will live and who will die? Who will die at his predestined time and who before his time?

As he came to the words: "who by water and *who*

Simcha's parents join us for a family portrait on Mount Zion.

by fire, I began to cry, and my thoughts returned to the dreadful day that was almost my last in this world. With tears streaming from my eyes, I joined the shouts of the congregation as we all affirmed that:

Repentance, Prayer, and Charity have the power to remove the evil decree!

Glossary

The following glossary provides a partial explanation of some of the Hebrew and Yiddish (Y.) words and phrases used in this book. The spellings and explanations reflect the way the specific word is used herein. Often, there are alternate spellings and meanings for the words.

AM YISRAEL: the People of Israel, the Jewish Nation.
ACHDUT: unity.

BARUCH HASHEM: "Thank God!"
BEIT KNESSET: a synagogue.
BERESHIT: Genesis, the first of the Five Books of Moses.
BITACHON: trust in God.
BEN TORAH: a learned, observant Jew.
B'EZRAT HASHEM: "With God's help!"

CHESED: acts of compassion and lovingkindness.
CHAZAN: a cantor; one who leads the prayer service.
CHALLAH (-LOT): braided Sabbath loaf (loaves).
CHAMETZ: leavened foods, prohibited during Passover.

DAVEN (Y.): to pray.

EREV SHABBAT: the day preceding Shabbos, i.e., Friday.
EMUNAH: faith in God.

HA-MELECH: the king.

IMMA: Mommy; mother.

KOHEN: a member of the priestly tribe.

KIDDUSH HASHEM: the sanctification of God.

KOL NIDREI: the opening prayer of the Yom Kippur service.

KOLLEL: a center for advanced Torah learning for adult students, mostly married men.

KOHELET: Ecclesiastes.

KIPPAH: a skullcap or yarmulke.

LAG BA-OMER: the 33rd day in the counting of the Omer, a festive day in the seven-week period of semi-mourning between Pesach and Shavuot.

MEGILLAT ESTHER: the Scroll of Esther, read on Purim.

MINYAN: a minimum of ten Jewish males aged 13 and over, the quorum required for congregational prayer.

MITZVAH: a Torah commandment.

MIDDAH (-DOT): (favorable) attribute(s).

MIDDAH K'NEGED MIDDAH: "measure for measure."

MELAVEH MALKAH: a festive meal on Saturday night to honor the departing "Sabbath queen."

OY VEY (Y.): "Woe is me!"

OY GEVALT (Y.): an outcry of despair.

RABBENU: our Teacher; our Master.

ROSH YESHIVAH: the dean of a YESHIVA.

ROSH CHODESH: the beginning of the Hebrew month.

REFUAH SHELEMAH: "[May you have] a complete recovery."

SH'LOM BAYIT: domestic peace and harmony.

SHIUR: a Torah lesson.

SHEMA: "Hear [O Israel]," the opening words of the fundamental prayer which proclaims the unity of God.

TEHILLIM: (the book of) Psalms.

UPSHEREN (Y.): the celebration of a three-year-old boy's first haircut.

VIDUI: confession; the confessional prayer recited before death.

YESHIVA: an academy of Torah study.

YETZER HA-RA: the Evil Inclination.

YAHRTZEIT (Y.): the anniversary of a death.

YOM TOV: a Jewish Festival.

THESE SHALL STAND FOR A BLESSING:

Jonathan, Laetitia, Liza and Julia Abramson
David Abramson, Carol Zimmerman, Daniel and Lily
Rabbi Gary Charlestein and family
Samuel and Norma Paige of Queens, New York

IN MEMORY OF
LEAH AND DAVID MOORE
by Malvina and Morton Charlestein

IN MEMORY OF MINNA SHAFTAN
by her daughter, Claire Ackerman

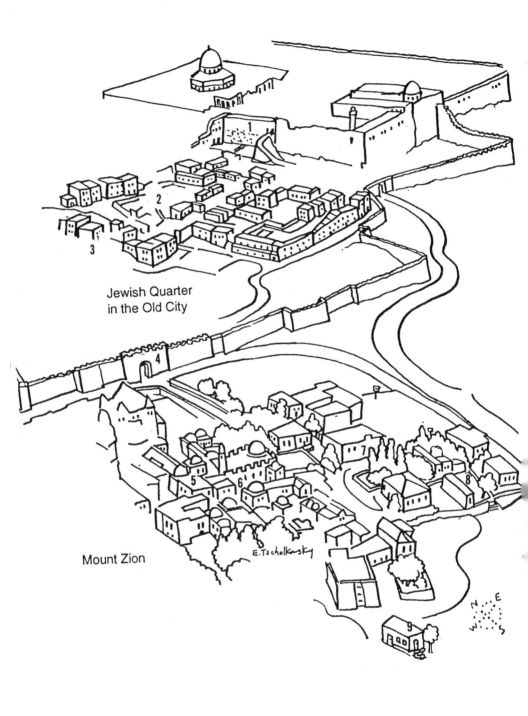

Jewish Quarter
in the Old City

Mount Zion

E. Tscholkovsky

N E
W S

1   Kotel Ha-Ma'aravi (Western Wall)
2   Churva Square
3   Ararat Street
4   Zion Gate
5   Upper Kollel apartments
6   King David's Tomb
7   Diaspora Yeshiva Study Hall
8   Lower Kollel
9   Women's Division

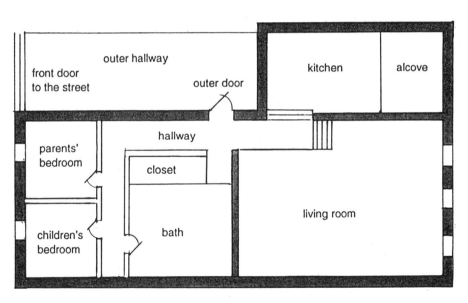

FLOOR PLAN OF THE ARARAT STREET APARTMENT